ELECTRIC EVANGELISM

ELECTRIC EVANGELISM

DENNIS C. BENSON

Nashville ABINGDON PRESS New York

ELECTRIC EVANGELISM

Copyright © 1973 by Dennis C. Benson

Library of Congress Cataloging in Publication Data

BENSON, DENNIS C. Electric evangelism.
1. Radio in religion. 2. Television in religion. I. Title.
BV656.B45   269'.2   72-7425

ISBN 0-687-11633-3

MANUFACTURED BY THE PARTHENON PRESS AT
NASHVILLE, TENNESSEE, UNITED STATES OF AMERICA

CONTENTS

I. WARNING: THIS BOOK IS DANGEROUS

In the hands of someone who does not love people —this is a dangerous book. There is a fine line between releasing the potentiality in people and manipulating them. If the reader who wants to use media creatively just moves the theological reference points over to the world of politics or economics, he will be able to gain results consistent with his goals. If he is selfish or exploitative, he can use people. I hope he will not. These thoughts are written in love to be used in love.

This book springs from working in media. The electric marketplace has been my life context. My learning has come from the people in the field. They have freely led me through an experiential education in mass media. Much of my time was spent with little financial support for the production of programming and media work. This will be a from-the-bottom-up kind of exploration into doing media with creativity and Christian sensitivity as your major tools.

The outflow of these pages may seem naïve to some. The folk who teach me are the most loving and trusting brothers and sisters with whom I have ever worked. In many cases, they have been more supportive than people I have met within traditional faith systems. This kind of perspective may run counter to all the articles you have read about mass media by ex-newsmen, politicians, and social commentators. However, I can only share with you the world I know.

This is not a book of complaint about how impossible it is to resist the electric age. It is true that there are demonic dimensions to mass media. However I have found these aspects in everything I have encountered. A creative response to the mind-set reflected in this book can enable you and your folk to do media with your local stations. If you put this book down with the hope of extending through mass media the love of Christ into others, we will have done what we set out to do. Once you admit the possibility of doing media yourself, your whole life will be different from what it was—so will your world. This is a dangerous book.

II. MASS MEDIA MEANDERING

A. MUDDLING IN MEDIA

There is usually a mixed reaction when someone starts talking about mass media. The electric culture is so seductive that it tends to lead "experts" into an intermix of language and thought which floats above reality. In other words, no one seems to understand quite what the media professional is talking about. Sometimes such a speaker doesn't know himself! Theology occasionally suffers from such a nonreality syndrome also.

At other times people get into an apocalyptic mindset and use the mass media as a "kick-me" for all the world's problems. It is true that the messenger has usually gotten the punishment for the undesired message. However, our electric circuitry is inseparable from the message it carries. It interprets, shapes, or massages its content. Our minds respond to the electric messengers in a certain way. We tend to let them entertain us as they deliver. In fact, we usually go to the radio or TV for a leisure mind-massage. A friend calls these modern communication webs "the chewing gum of the mind."

These observations apply not only to our times. We can recognize such realities in the history of faith systems. People have often been enamored of style and form at the expense of the message. Paul seemed to dazzle the folk gathered at Mars Hill with his reasoning and examples. However it was the form that they admired in his preaching. He was restless with the results. Many a modern preacher has moved a congregation to tears with an emotional illustration, only to have them forget why he used it. Great Christian communicators have won reputations for their use of language and dramatic power. However, people have been hard put to remember what they were saying— at least, the devoted listeners carried away the strong impression of the medium.

This may not be so bad. The Christian faith is a curious mix of medium and message. We have probably been a bit too linear or language-oriented in transmitting the faith within and without the church.

B. MEDIATOR AS MEDIUM

Jesus reached out and stroked his listeners with an experience which made the Word of God incarnate in their midst. Scripture suggests that many layers of the Good News touched people where they were. Even the youngest and most unsophisticated listener could be enwrapped in the love of God as it took flesh in their midst. The medium (Jesus) and the message (the Good News) were inseparable.

I remember watching a film which was being shown without the sound track turned on. We were trying to sensitize ourselves to the body rhythms of the two people in the movie. One lady sat and watched me instead of the film. After the screening, she explained that she had been deaf at one point in her life. She was now drawn to watch lips move, and this would have kept her from really watching the body language. She had decided to watch the film through me. She then went on to explain what the film was about from what I had projected to her.

Many people can recall the love and goodness of a special Sunday school teacher. His or her message may be lost in the cobwebs of the past, but the form he gave that message by his life remains. Maybe the Christian community should more fully appreciate the fact that the world is very sensitive to the interrelationship between form and content. Public schools have been slow to embrace this reality. The tightly packaged form of an academic discipline may destroy the excitement and depth of the content. In many cases the medium used to extend a message may be more impressive than the content itself.

The folk creating our mass media have been aware of the new wine-wineskin relationship. Great care has been put into the formulation of our entertainment and commercial input. They know that the message is that which touches. Too many Sunday school teachers have been caught shouting down the noisy class in the last minutes of the lesson. After they have violently forced them to be quiet, they have the students repeat that day's message: "God is Love." The early church ran into these kinds of problems. People would comment on the nature of the medium. To some the Spirit-filled disciples seemed like "drunken men." Others were moved because the Christians showed the world "how much they love each other."

Faith people have an essence. They come from somewhere with something. If they are going to share what or who is in them, they must be entrenched in the message. Many Christian folk do not know what it is they are called to share or be. The temptation is to simplify the message. This is a good communication principle. However, it is also dangerous. A one-minute summary of the faith is not going to encompass the whole scope of salvation. Yet, such discipline of compressing thought will be needed in the electric media maze.

It is equally important to know the folk who are to receive the message. Who is "Massmediaman"? Simplification again can be dangerous. We have often used very limited outward marks of the man to know him. Our input has often been restricted to job and education kinds of classification. There are other ways of getting into a man's life. Radio and television stations are using some interesting ways of finding where the audience is. We will touch on this important area again.

Most of all, the churchman must understand the fabric from which his wineskin must be cut. The electric maze is different from the media he has used in the past. It resists the kind of translation he has undertaken before. The churchman may simply take what has been done in the one medium over to the new form. For instance, it is a temptation to broadcast the worship service as it stands. The radio transmission of the corporate experience of celebration takes on some new, strange messages in radioland. The participatory involvement of being a gathered community just doesn't come across on the radio. Even a TV presentation of the service delivers a different message from the original form.

It is the capacity to intermix message, audience, and medium which enables people to embrace an existence of meaning and giving in the electric age. The state of religious broadcasting suggests that the Christian church has not effectively passed this threshold of incarnation. There have been, and are, moments of genuine communication of the Good News through mass media. However, the only hope for making an impact on man in medialand is the possibility that the local person will undertake this kind of media ministry. National offices of religious media can give us flashes of hope. In the long pull, however, it is you and your folk who will make the difference.

C. MASSMEDIAMAN

The broadcasting or proclamation of the Good News has always been the thrust of what the church has called evangelism. The Word preached has been a core of meaning for most strains of Christian tradition. In recent times, this focus has been shunned, neglected, or distorted. Most often church folk have treated this living extension of the faith as a linear function. As long as the religious words have been muttered, the evangel could feel his responsibility fulfilled.

The middle-aged church member kept shaking his head. We were talking about the girl who had left home for a life which included drugs, an abortion, and stealing. "She knew what was right. She had heard the Good News and rejected it. There is only hell for her." Nothing could dissuade him from his judgment. Unfortunately, it isn't that simple. Maybe she had experienced the loving person of Jesus Christ, and maybe she hadn't. Just because she had been in church from her early years doesn't mean that she had encountered the Word of life. This is not to say that a revival series in the church would have assured her salvation. The one who is called (that is all of us in the faith) to bear the Word to others can never experience the satisfaction, with total confidence, that he has finished his job.

There is something deep and flowing about the ministry of Christ which keeps shaking up the lives of those who are touched. Peter, on the road to his Jerusalem ministry, is pointed to a broader understanding of God's people (including the Gentiles). Paul is turned around again and again. The history of the brothers and sisters in the faith shows God leading his people in many directions. If we are using the same structures for worship, study, outreach, and fellowship in our community that were used fifteen years ago, something is wrong. During this same span of time most major corporations have changed several times in their marketing, managing, and accounting procedures. The world has changed in life-mode numerous times during this period. The fermenting nature of our message keeps expanding those who bear it. The change of the world nicely meets the expansive nature of the message. Yet, most faith communities are not using new wineskins.

Having watched and produced hundreds of religious radio and TV shows, I don't think that religion can be broadcast. The lumpy nature of linear religious chunks thrown into most station formats causes media indigestion. The depth of the message is eroded by the inconsistent forms we use for the media presentation. The only place for the rigid religious programming of the past is the Sunday morning ghetto. Here it reaches those who are already within the faith community. This kind of reinforcement of existing faith is useful and needed. However, such an approach does not fulfill the radical demand to go out and preach the Good News to those far and near. The unsaved of the world are not being touched by such insular communication attempts.

At the same time, I have no doubt at all that the spiritual hunger of Massmediaman can be nurtured with a richness as never before—through mass media. The electric age has created a fanastic longing for love and meaning.

The old pensioner sits alone and watches his TV set. His family and loved ones are not living in his town. He views and experiences a world of activity and celebration. It interests him. It arouses his humanity. It makes him crave to touch others in community. Yet, the media can only tease. The ads usually offer satisfaction through the products offered. However, nothing can substitute for human interaction, which the media doesn't provide.

The models and probes of media ministry in this book may seem heavily weighted with a humanistic concern. They are. I believe that the two natures of Christ (Son of God and Son of man) have always been two parts of a total truth. At certain times in the thrust of Christian history, one aspect of the Christ has been the needed Good News at the expense of the other. Heresy, in terms of orthodox theology, lurks near by. However, it seems that God permits the gift of the divine or human Christ to be received as it is needed in the context of a given time. The 70s suggest that our society is crying for the humanity of Christ. Rather than fearing heresy or demanding only the divine aspect of the two natures, it seems most fitting to let the world have the Christ of Scripture. He was truly man also. Our world is pleading to know God's love through its humanity. So far we have not done our job very well.

At first, modern Christianity wandered through a lot of social action. I really felt called when I marched with Dr. Martin Luther King, Father Groppi, Dr. William Coffin, and others. If the times were the same again, I would probably be there. However, it was not enough to get at the problem in that way. We didn't always embrace the full implications of Dr. King's non-violence and love. The commercial world has made an ersatz attempt at giving us the human Christ we desire. How else can the cults of Jesus which flourish around record albums, stage plays, films, etc., be explained? The new subcultures are another mark of people seeking Jesus as the Son of man. The Jesus movement is an interesting expression of this theological phenomenon. These are signs of human needs.

I believe that the source of knowing the total Christ must come from those embracing both the humanity and the divinity of Jesus. Folk rooted in such a view are then free enough to enable others to know the faith without distortion through the medium of humanity. Those who have experienced the whole picture can best share the portion of the design which will communicate at the place where a person must start his understanding.

Yet, it has been very hard for church people to let our Lord take flesh among us. Our pictures of the

Christ are dramatic presentations from the 1920s. When he smiles, it is a patronizing upturn of the mouth directed to those below. When he suffers, he looks as if he were in some soap drama. I can not really share in his suffering through this art. A lot of Christian people seem not to want "God with us." They think it better that he stay away and remain a divine image. The press of spiritually hungry people may be God acting upon the people of faith, forcing them to re-examine their attitude toward the humanity of Christ.

D. HOLY SPIRIT AND MASS MEDIA

At first sight it might seem hopeless. We are caught in the bind of transition. Good folks don't want to commit themselves radically to a faith which may leave us with nothing but Christ. Our trappings are important. It is frightening to be stripped of every bit of security except our relationship to Jesus and his community.

This is not to deny the force and necessity of history. Without history we lose community and faith. We have faith because of those who have been lifted up before us. However, there is a difference between history and nostalgia. Nostalgia is a homesickness for our remembered experience. History is rooted in a reality which transcends our dreams about the past. Nostalgia can often be the glue which connects us with our heritage. However, nostalgia can be an emotional crutch which keeps us from facing the present and future with the same strength we had in the past. One man's history is another man's nostalgia. The Christian message is history. Its proclamation is now. The intersection of history (message) and the now (proclamation) is the occasion of the Holy Spirit's manifestation.

In fact, this age is the season of the Holy Spirit. The electric environment prepares people for the kinds of experience and communication which we have often attributed to the Holy Spirit at other times. Yet, the faith community could not have created a popular experience of our Lord such as *Jesus Christ Superstar*. We do not seem to have the creative Spirit-energy to be released. We did not manifest our Jesus as well as the world did. To spend our time quibbling over the failure is a sign of spiritual bankruptcy. We are a wandering community asking everywhere, "What have they done with our Jesus?" It may be God's judgment upon the church body, because it has failed to nurture our people's spiritual hunger. However, in the course of the church's history, extreme revisionist movements have not been the final solution. The cults and sects have forced the orthodox position to understand its abuse of the faith. The general folk of the world do not embrace offshoots built around one aspect of the faith. In fact, the elitism of religious extremism often offends those most in need of the message.

In spite of these critical remarks, I am totally secure in saying that the most creative body on earth today is the church. I have met more open-spirited folk in the American church than anywhere else in our society. They come in all kinds of theological shapes and forms. Their ages span the calendar. Some bear labels like conservative and radical. Many of these folk are buried deep in the heartland of the country. These folk are often a remnant within the larger body. They are misunderstood and little rewarded. Abuse from their brothers and sisters is not uncommon. However, I think that these folk are going to turn the society upside down with the creative teaching of the faith. They are so much into their message (it is so much into them), and they love their people so deeply that they will risk anything—anything—to bring Christ and their people together.

The place where you find this kind of ferment is most often among religious educators. Yes, in that same Sunday school there is a revolution going on. You may not have seen it yet. It is just beginning to peek out. I hope that you are one of these restless folk. Most of my work has been with these local people in the past few years. They are now bringing a new awakening in their immediate circle of influence. However, in the course of this short book, I am going to suggest the next staging area for radical love and faith: mass media. In the past, much space has been filled with a kind of critique which ultimately forces the reader to think that the electric web is "out there." It is "way out." However, there is unlimited opportunity to do media in your own community. You can virtually take over mass media outlets. The need for your creativity and sensitivity is overwhelming. This area of concern may warrant your whole time of personal ministry. More is at stake in the mass media apostolate than in many local churches. Many congregations have focused in on themselves or their immediate neighborhood. However, Christ calls his followers to reach out to the world with his message. We have never before had the opportunity which is now ours.

One of the most difficult aspects of your media ministry will be to bring others along with you. Unfortunately most pastors don't look at mass media in the way we are suggesting. They have been trained in a very linear, or print, tradition. What usually happens is that one person in the community may understand the power and importance of electric media. He will then take it all for himself. There is a huge ego factor in doing radio and TV. There is nothing wrong with getting satisfaction from a media experience. However, if this enjoyment robs others of the chance to share their religious gifts, something is wrong. If a churchman can carry along with him the support of the whole religious community (ministerium, ministerial groups, councils of churches, etc.), he will have an even better avenue to a station. They like to be assured that the whole religious community is being served. This is right. On a public medium there is no place for highly parochial messages. At best, we are only creating a climate or a setting within which the real work of the message can take place. This also means that you might have to undertake this kind of ministry on your own. Others in the community will simply say that they don't have time. This is always an interesting comment. It suggests priorities. I hope that one of your important areas of work will be mass media. In most cases the ecumenical group will be glad to turn this dimension of Christian outreach over to you. Just remember your responsibility to enable others to do media.

The style of ministry suggested in these pages is not built on money or special training. You must be into your faith. You must be freed by Christ to risk for others and his message. You must be willing to learn through experience. You must be ready to rechannel your thinking, while utilizing all the experience which the church has given you in the past. You must. Without you, there will be nothing of hope in the electric marketplace.

III. THE MASS MEDIA MAZE

A. THE SYSTEM

Radio and television stations are imposing organizations. We come to them as fans. They sound so permanent, or is it just that we have depended on them for so long? The stations seem to own airwaves or channels. There are good reasons for our feeling. A company or organization owns the station. This is underscored again and again in our relationship to the station. It is their station. The station is housed in their facilities. These studios and offices may be very extensive, or ridiculously scant. But we have been conditioned to accept the independent business person as the one who has the last say in his own operation. After all, he is the one who has organized and built what is his.

Stations, however, are different from other businesses in some respects. In the first place, they are only using "your" airwaves. The federal government gives them permission or licenses for the operation of their programming on certain assigned airwaves. The broadcast space belongs to you. Every three years each station must apply for the renewal of its license. Part of their rationale for existence is service to your community. The Federal Communications Commission supposedly watchdogs the stations of the country to see that things are not broadcast that are not in the best interest of the community. This founding ideal has been challenged from time to time.

In one sense the industry is very sensitive to this responsibility. However, in another sense they really feel that they own the station, and the public is just an audience. Sometimes the FCC applies muscle in a bad situation. However, I don't think that local folk should depend on the FCC complaint route as a means of making an impact on the mass media outlets. I say this despite the fact that in some cases local groups, with some national church support, have gotten some remarkable results in cases where stations were violating good broadcasting standards. Everett Parker of the United Church of Christ has done a fantastic job of helping citizen groups police their airwaves.

It is regrettable that many churchmen respond to something they don't like on their local station by writing a threatening letter. Usually they will wave a complaint to the FCC before the program manager's face. I can concede that some gross injustice to the people in the community may warrant the stiffest action possible. However, this is not the course of action we are going to pursue here. We are more interested in doing programming over a long period of time with a station.

It is very useful to visit your station when the license-renewal times come around. You may even be contacted for a report on the needs of the community. Ask your contact when the license will be available for public viewing. It must be available to the public for a prescribed period of time when renewal time comes, but nobody ever looks at a license in most communities. Make it clear to your contact person that you just want to get acquainted with their goals and values, and don't make any comments when you and a lawyer friend visit for the viewing. Don't be surprised if there is an obvious case of nerves from those around the station. They are always afraid that someone might challenge them for the license. Such a course in seeking information is important. You will know what they have promised to do in the next three years. Some students of media claim that no station ever really lives up to its promises. This may be an overstatement. However, the fact that you know what they promised and they know that you know will take a lot of emotional pressure off the situation. A creative power lever will replace a destructive, suspicious relationship.

Let's say that your media-oriented folk monitor a station or check their logs and find that they are not able to program the percentage of public service time they have promised. You can walk into the station and tell them that you have noticed that they are having trouble doing what they have planned in public service. Your group can then offer them four or five program ideas which you have designed. There will be no need for pressure or threats. Information can greatly reduce the kind of emotional situations which have filled our recent history when special interest groups

encounter each other. It is fear and the lack of know-
ledge which breed distrust.

A station is in business to make money. They also
want to keep their license. To make money, they have
to win an audience. These factors are important to
your understanding of broadcasting. I have found that
these aspects of self-interest move around in terms of
priority. The media folk are not just money-hungry
bloodsuckers as they have been popularly character-
ized in the recent past. In fact, at certain times (like
at license renewal) good public service programming
is most important. At other times a solid audience
rating is the most important factor for a station. Upon
the audience rests the station's finances. They get advertising and set rates according to the station's position in the media market.

It is ironic that the church has most often tried to
buy its way into a station. Just buying times doesn't
insure much. Our real strength is our ability to know
the needs and concerns of the community. We also
have the gift of creative outlook as a result of our faith.
At least, these *should* be the strengths of the churchman. In some cases, unfortunately, we can collect
money better than we can probe the center of people's
lives. Creativity has not been the mark of the church
in recent years. This is an asset greatly demanded in
the media world. Most of the creative media people
just don't have time to extend this side of their nature
to public service programming.

B. MEDIA FOLK

I hate to sound so naïve. However, I must confess
that I relate to the mass media people as if they were
honest, understanding, and concerned with the com-

munity. My stance is based on the relationships of the past few years. Too many critics of mass media approach the media people as if they were the worst breed of humankind on earth. With this attitude, I am not surprised when this is the kind of person they find. The Christian doesn't have to arm himself with this kind of suspicion. We are free in Christ, and we know that Jesus died for the release of every man. Every person is my brother, and I am free to approach him in love and peace. I think that this unique Christian approach to man enables a flow of good vibes. It is true that man is sinful and prone to be selfish. However, Christ gives us the hope of redemption and forgiveness as we acknowledge and actualize his community.

I guess part of the good experience I have had with producers, directors, technicians, station managers, and other talent is because I came to mass media knowing nothing about it. My academic background simply didn't prepare me for the electric maze. Instead of playing expert, I just came open and empty. There is something disarming about honesty. I have learned so much so quickly. I was working as the director of a youth ministry for a Catholic-Protestant organization in a large mass market area. When our director of communications left, I was asked to step into the job. I hadn't had a day of formal training in media. I refused the job on several occasions. Then John Bucker, acting chairman of the communication department, and W. Lee Hicks, director of the organization, encouraged me to take the leap. I can vaguely remember standing in the studio. I had only been in our production facilities a few times. Wires and tubes are not my thing. It seemed that tapes and cords were hanging down from every piece of equipment. There

I stood. It suddenly hit me. The twelve radio and TV shows were due at the end of the week. I called a half-dozen high school students from my circle of friends and told them that we were in trouble. They said, "What do you mean *we* are in trouble?" However, they came over, and we learned through our risks and the help given to us by the media folk.

You will learn a lot quickly. There are many givens around which you must work. Your director and producer (often one and the same) are in control. It is hard for a clergyman to take direction. It is good for him, though. Time is the biggest enemy of those in media. The professionals just don't have the time you do. You may think that you are busy, but one day at the side of any local director or producer will shame you. In fact, I feel that limited time is the factor which may be robbing the media of much potentiality.

The mass media creator must work in linear fashion. He needs scripts, logs, permission notes, etc. But these traditional structural patterns simply don't blend easily with the random nature of electric media. A show can be technically created on the spot. It can capture reality as it becomes. However, in most situations time and equipment limitation (including breakdowns) do not permit immediate, live production. The slotting of work times and union coffee breaks may often squeeze the media out of their own wineskins. A news anchor man may be just two paragraphs from the end of a story when the segment time runs out, and he must smoothly sign off. Marshall McLuhan has suggested that the media are running themselves. If some person were running it all, it would be easy to correct the things that are wrong about your TV and radio programs. Just fire the guy in charge.

The folk in this profession know that they are caught

in the squeeze. When you dump your righteous anger on them about something you don't like, you reveal two things to them. In the first place, you are saying that you don't really understand what they are facing as producers or talent in mass media. In the second place, you are continuing the negativism of our time. Sure, you could produce a better program than the one you didn't like last week. However, where would you be on program number seventy-eight in the series? It is to the shame of the church that most of our criticism about mass media is mere second-guessing. Anyone can be critical. However, I think that the Christian is particularly equipped by faith to participate in the "new creation." Creativity is inseparable from our faith commitment. Frequently when Christians start suggesting ideas for programming it becomes even worse. They simply haven't thought through the implications for the real world of the verbal faith commitments they have made.

Most media people have had bad experiences with religious folk. When they are Christians themselves, they usually share a limited concept of what the faith can convey on the tube or over the airwaves. We have conditioned them to see the Christian experience as being linear and limiting. When they have had an opportunity to pick up the vibrations from a local churchman, they expect some ego trip exposure for his own church, or programming fit only for the Sunday morning ghetto. This means that they will not expect very much from you. You will have to win their respect and confidence. They are being hyped by a dozen forces every day. The media game is hard and competitive. You survive by being careful. This gives the Christian a great opportunity to provide the kind of trusting relationship which cannot be found very easily in the trade. You will find a great ministry of nurture and care to the station people.

It is amazing how much need for this kind of acceptance there is among these electric folk. You can easily become a chaplain/confessor to the employees, once you have established the sharing relationship. Station people come and go rapidly. It is a hard life. The security is shaky. Someone with a solid base of inner security can be a great contribution to the station mix. Though some of the station personnel may be church members with Christian commitments, this factor in itself does not assure anything. The typical transition of religious experience into the job area of mass media is not very encouraging.

What has been said about the radio and television people could fit almost any vocation. However, I think there is an acute degree of personal exposure in the media game. You are the medium on radio and television. Public reaction can lift and/or destroy personal confidence. The highs and the lows are unnatural and distorted. The degree of personal manifestation of the Good News in our lives will determine the kind of success we will have. The Christian has something of depth to give. We must be anchored in a kind of security and freedom that will enable station folk to be creative. There is no substitute for authenticity in the media bag. We have to be real in order to make it with these folk. The Word should live in us and we in the Word. No set religious words are called for in this kind of ministry. What we need is the linkage between ourselves and our message.

A lot of the programming which needs to be done by most stations cannot be done by present station personnel. The newsmen, jocks, and air personalities in most situations cannot probe the dimension of man in the manner required by the times. That talent can be provided by the religious community. The professionals respect those who can do their speciality well. This is particularly true when you are not trying to compete for existing jobs. The fact that you are coming to local media work in most cases without pay is vital. To be accepted as a colleague without competing against them is a great position.

Finally, media people have been worn down by repeated criticism. Two or three critical letters disturb them more than they should. They are somewhat like the preacher who will worry all week because word has reached him that "somebody" is upset over last week's sermon. His insecurity and lack of feedback will distort this criticism out of its proper perspective. The uncertain mass media job security tends to give criticism too much importance. The Christian approach of love and understanding will result in a response in kind. These are good folk. They need to release their potentiality.

C. MEDIA OVERLOAD

I must also warn you about another factor in the world you are about to enter as participant. It is one thing to watch television or listen to radio. Your mind is being massaged. However, your head is being overhauled from inside when you are the messenger. In another place (*Electric Liturgy* [Richmond: John Knox Press, 1972]) I have chronicled my own electric addiction in the midst of media. The closer you get to doing media the more you realize that you are dealing with deep extensions of your energy. It is probably much like a drug experience. The media age has created a new level of energy which tends to overload those who are closest to it. You just can't conduct the power alone.

This is one explanation for the fast incineration of the new stars which burn across the pop music sky. They come on quickly and burn out rapidly (Hendrix, Joplin, Morrison, and others). Recently, I sat in the hockey locker room which served as a dressing room for Joe Cocker and his support people. I finally made my way to Joe. It was a bit frightening. The concert had been on the road for seven weeks. The cast of thirty who support Joe on stage were happy and relieved. Tomorrow they would return to London for a week of rest. Then it would be back to Los Angeles and some recording. Members of the group walked up to Joe and comforted him. He sat on the player's bench in a daze. Beads of sweat appeared on his face then ran down his skin into his soaked shirt. I asked if I could interview him briefly. He just smiled faintly and offered no resistance. Every probe resulted in vague mumbling from the rock and roll star. He seemed stunned and unable to comprehend what was going on. The superstars of the age must conduct the electric energy of the music they create. They are used as substitute embodiments of the emotions and romance of the time. Most of them have to insulate themselves from the fans. They just can't handle it.

Church people working with mass media won't be pressured by the demands of electric superstars. However, there is an overload dimension to media ministries. The usual Sunday preaching schedule, which many pastors have experienced as pressure, will seem minor compared to the demands of producing for mass media. You can't recycle old sermons or fake a time slot when you are in a tight format. This is particularly

true when the programming demands several components. It must all come together in spite of technical
failures, human frailties, and the press of time.

One Friday evening we had just finished editing a
complex radio show for airing on Saturday morning. In
the process of cleaning up the studio one of our producers erased the tape. The inner cry of agony I felt
can only be known by someone who has seen such a
tragedy unfold. I stayed there all night building a new
show out of nothing. I called back the host and had
him lay down voice tracks of questions asked of a
guest he had never met. I took answers of the guest
which had been recorded for another show two years
before. To add to my trouble, I needed to stretch the
interview to fit the Saturday morning format. The host
had to pad the questions. The two conversations then
had to be edited together and the introduction and
conclusion produced from previous tapes. It was a
hard day's night.

This kind of environment is what the media man
works in continually. The flow and rhythm of the Good
News as you incarnate it must be in sync with this
kind of energy demand. The people of this world are
sitting on top of an excellent opportunity for new un-
derstandings of theology in our age.

IV. DOING RADIO: SOMETHING FOR THE HOLES IN YOUR HEAD

Just about everyone has experienced radio. It is the electric medium that cuts across the life-span of everyone living. Some folk remember the golden days of radio drama and strong personalities. The nostalgia bug has even introduced this dimension of radio to the young. However, radio is different from what it used to be. In fact, most of the old-time radio fans would go crazy if they were locked in a room with eight hours of pioneer radio. They have been changed with the times.

A. THE INSIDE OUT

Radio programming is now carefully formatted to communicate to a particular audience. At least, this is what happens. We listen to particular stations in order to receive the kinds of sounds we desire. Some listeners will not stray from the top-forty or the rock station. There are those who like the all-talk format, which is now appearing in some cities. In major media markets you find soul (or ethnic), country and western, middle of the road (MOR), underground, and classical formats. Something for everybody.

Formatted radio has done much to change the time clock within us. Regardless of whether the rapidly segmented input of information—news, time, music, ads, etc.—reflects the society or has influenced it, we are different from what we were in the past because of it. Just log a radio station of your liking for an hour or so. Each new segment should be entered in your journal. You will be amazed to see anywhere from twenty to thirty bits of input within the half-hour. This small aspect of radio programming suggests a radical change in our way of thinking. Just imagine what happens when we move from the stimulation of varied input in short segments to long blocks of information. Educational, social, and religious institutions must fight just to overcome the metabolism gap between the two input processes.

Program directors rise and fall on the basis of their formula for the station's sound. At least, that is how they are judged. If their particular combination of music selection, jock approach, and continuity flow gets good numbers in the rating books, they are geniuses. If the numbers drop or another station overtakes them, the program gets axed for failing to come up with the right sound. Some media observers question whether it is the combination of sound which wins listeners or not. Others don't have much faith in the numbers game. The samplings can be erratic and limited. However, this is the way the game is run. The churchman had better understand it. In the past we have not, and this can be the only explanation for those hairy blocks of religious input which create such stoppage in the middle of a station's regular format.

It was an announcer's meeting. The program director was conducting a serious analysis of another station's format for his staff. "Why has the station picked up this section of the audience profile?" The silence was heavy. Everyone was trying to catch the nuance of format which made the difference. Then the program director diagrammed the log from a typical hour. He then used a felt marker to underscore the talk inputs. This log was compared to that of their own station. The red marks revealed that the successful station had less talk at key points in the hour. This kind of close scrutiny goes on at every good station.

On the basis of format alone most religious programming will not be aired during prime listening times. No program director will want to break up the format for a religious block. Until recently the typical religious program was made up of preaching and music, and that just doesn't fit into a schedule where the general audience is listening. This is not a rejection of our message—but of the form we have always chosen.

Much radio programming by the church is for a very specialized audience. The broadcast of preaching and church music will be popular with those who already like it. There is nothing wrong with such specialized formats. However, it does not reach those who are without this kind of orientation. It also seems futile to aim at a few shut-ins in a local community by using a medium with the capability of such a vast audience.

The audio cassette or some other specialized medium would seem much more to the point for such nurture.

It may seem a bit inside out to start with people. However, there is no other way to do communication in mass media. Every station tries to focus on the audience it would like to have. Some stations are using extensive sampling techniques to determine the needs, goals, interests, and resources of their audience. They want to touch the lives of their listeners. The stations want to win the loyalty of their audience. Some stations employ research techniques which measure audiences by life-style. Thev contend that you can't tell the inner pace of a person's life from educational, vocational, or social marks. They know that a thirteen-year-old boy may love Lawrence Welk, while his seventy-five-year-old grandmother is a Rolling Stones freak. Modern society has experienced a disintegration of stereotyped personalities. Everyone is forging his own selfhood for a number of different reasons.

Theologically, the modern Christian has been uncomfortable concerning the state of the person needing the Good News. Humanism has been a touchy subject. This wasn't always the case. As we have suggested, the fact of the Incarnation of the Word underscores God's affirmation of human existence. The early church changed the world because it met the world where it was. It took seriously the life situation of a man confronting the Christ. Greek and Hebrew Christians seem to have needed different apostles and different idioms in order to receive the basic message. This was hard for the fathers in the faith. However, the book of Acts gives us an amazing picture of diversity in unity.The church utilized the communication patterns of its people. Humanity was the cradle for the nurture of faith.

It will be most helpful for our discussion if we keep focusing on mass media through a cross-section view of the people. Who is the person receiving our message? Any generalization is dangerous. People simply aren't old, middle-aged, young adult, and youth. However, stations have to look at and for audiences. We need some hooking places from which we can get a grip on mass media.

B. WORSHIP AND MASS MEDIA

As has been suggested, worship is a difficult experience to translate into the electric medium. I have experienced worship events in which electric media have been used. Some of these have been mind-boggling, as when fourteen-thousand people stood and linked hands together as a community. I have seen it happen around the stimulation of electric media experiences involving Pete Seeger, The Who, and *Jesus Christ Superstar*. These events generated much of the excitement and community one feels from reading Acts 2. This is not to say that these entertainers are necessarily messengers of the Holy Spirit. However, our response to them was very much like the manifestations the church experienced in the camp-meeting religion of the past.

My wife Marilyn and I were driving back from Detroit. We had left the children with grandparents and were ready for the week in Florida. It would be seven days of sharing with media folk from all over the world. The World Association of Christian Communicators was having its annual North American section meeting. The travel arrangements were such that we didn't attend services that Sunday morning. I finally found a strong signal on the car radio. What we heard the next twenty minutes was unbelievable. The ministerial voice on the radio told us to bow our heads in prayer. This was fine for his people. However, it would have been disastrous for those of us in cars. During the offering there was dead air. Apparently the service was miked in such a way that the musical selection couldn't be heard by the radio worshipers. When the minister came to the announcements, we learned that the tape was two weeks old. He was inviting us to meetings and church affairs which were now past. One should always be charitable concerning the mistakes and difficulties which people have in leading worship. However, what that service said to us was that it was not really directed to us. It was an elitist in-thing to which we were allowed to listen from the outside. The Good News was not being proclaimed to us. It belonged to someone else, somewhere else.

Let's suppose that your church is trapped in the Sunday morning ghetto with a broadcast service. There are some things you can do with what you have to sharpen the impact of your outreach. Beg your church officers to tape the show and delay it by a week. There are some arguments you can use. Tell them that this will save the charges usually paid by the church for live broadcast. Indicate to your brothers and sisters in power that this additional time can help you improve the impact of the worship service for those outside. If you have been able to accomplish this change, buy yourself a tape-editing block, I use an S-3 Editall for this, and I am prejudiced in favor of this little piece of machined aluminum. A good electronics store can order it for around ten dollars, so don't buy some of the cheaper ones. Professionals use a precision tape editor. With this small piece of aluminum, a razor blade, and some editing tape, you can reshape the whole service.

Audio tape is very easily edited by cutting and splicing. I have trained fourteen- and fifteen-year-old students to be expert editors. With just a little practice, you can remove an entire segment of material, or only the audible pop of lips parting before a word is spoken. Just find the position of the playback head on your reel-to-reel tape recorder. Use a china marker (we used to call them grease pencils) to mark the places on the tape where corrections are desired. You should indicate where the editing is to begin and end. Using one of the slots on the edit block, cut the audio tape on the marks. If you are just removing a bit, move the cut ends of the tape together from either side of the excized piece. The ends should just touch. Then a half-inch piece of edit tape on the shiny side of the audio tape will seal the cut. If you are a bit careful, no one will ever know something has been removed. And, of course, things can be put in as well as taken out, and the position of materials changed around (see the illustrations of this process).

You can take this simple skill and create a service which will meet the needs of those listening. There are a number of worship segments which have no meaning to the man on the road or in his home. Perhaps you should reduce the service to fifteen minutes instead of the hour. Remember how the chronology of regular programming moves rapidly from one thing to the next. Perhaps you could include the call to worship, a hymn, Scripture, and edited sermon with closing prayer and hymn. In most cases the use of an edit block would improve the sermons we preach and listen to each week. It would be interesting to see what worshipers would do if they had to edit a sermon

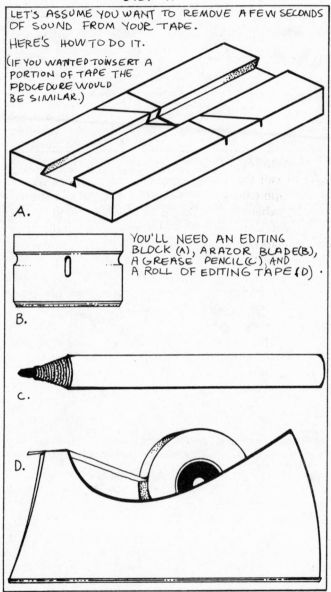

LET'S ASSUME YOU WANT TO REMOVE A FEW SECONDS
OF SOUND FROM YOUR TAPE.

HERE'S HOW TO DO IT.

(IF YOU WANTED TO INSERT A
PORTION OF TAPE THE
PROCEDURE WOULD
BE SIMILAR.)

A.

YOU'LL NEED AN EDITING
BLOCK (A), A RAZOR BLADE (B),
A GREASE PENCIL (C), AND
A ROLL OF EDITING TAPE (D).

B.

C.

D.

STEP 2.

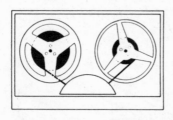

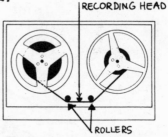

RECORDING HEAD

ROLLERS

RECORDER WITH GUARD IN
PLACE

RECORDER WITH RECORDING
HEAD EXPOSED

THERE IS PROBABLY SOME SORT OF GUARD OVER THE
RECORDING HEAD OF YOUR TAPE RECORDER. IF THIS GUARD
PREVENTS YOUR EASY ACCESS TO THE HEAD, YOU'D
BETTER TAKE IT OFF DURING YOUR EDITING. USUALLY
THIS IS A SIMPLE MATTER OF REMOVING A FEW SCREWS.

STEP 3.

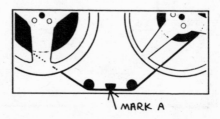

MARK A

FIND THE BEGINNING OF THE SECTION OF TAPE YOU
WANT TO REMOVE. FIND THE APPROXIMATE POINT BY
RUNNING THE TAPE AT PROPER SPEED. ZERO IN ON
THE EXACT POINT BY PULLING THE TAPE ACROSS THE
HEAD BY HAND. IT WON'T TAKE LONG FOR YOU TO GET
THE KNACK. MARK THE POINT (MARK A) ON THE
SHINY SIDE OF THE TAPE (THE BACKING) WITH YOUR
GREASE PENCIL.

40

STEP 4.

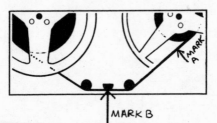

MARK B

NOW FIND THE END OF THE SECTION YOU WANT TO REMOVE (MARK B). MARK IT WITH YOUR GREASE PENCIL.

STEP 5.

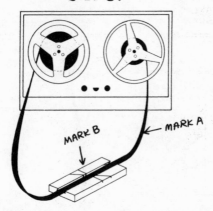

MARK B   MARK A

NOW PRESS THE TAPE INTO THE GROOVE OF THE EDITING BLOCK, SHINY SIDE UP. MARK B SHOULD BE EXACTLY OVER THE SLOT THAT RUNS DIAGONALLY ACROSS THE BLOCK. CUT THE TAPE ACROSS THE DIAGONAL SLOT WITH YOUR RAZOR. THERE IS ALSO A SLOT RUNNING STRAIGHT ACROSS THE BLOCK, BUT THIS IS USED ONLY WHERE EXTREME ACCURACY IS NECESSARY, SINCE THE SPLICE IT MAKES ISN'T AS STRONG AS THE DIAGONAL ONE.

41

STEP 6.

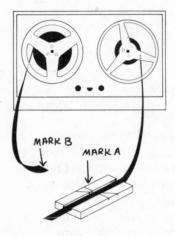

MARK B   MARK A

NOW MOVE THE TAPE IN
THE SLOT TO MARK A.
MAKE YOUR DIAGONAL
CUT. DISCARD THE
WASTE TAPE.

STEP 7.

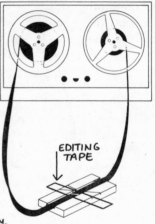

EDITING
TAPE

FIT THE TWO ENDS OF THE
TAPE TOGETHER IN THE
SLOT OF THE BLOCK.
BE SURE THERE ARE
NO TWISTS IN THE TAPE.
PLACE A PIECE OF
EDITING TAPE OVER
THE SPLICE AS SHOWN
AND PRESS IT FIRMLY
DOWN.

STEP 8.
TRIM OFF THE EXCESS EDITING
TAPE WITH YOUR RAZOR AND
YOU HAVE ACCOMPLISHED YOUR AIM.
YOU HAVE EDITED YOUR TAPE AS
YOU INTENDED.

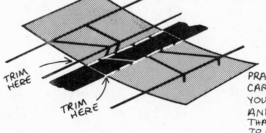

TRIM
HERE

TRIM
HERE

PRACTICE AND
CARE WILL MAKE
YOUR SPLICES RIGHT
AND TOUGH. AND
THAT'S ALL THERE IS
TO IT.

42

down to the one most important minute. Both listener and preacher would learn a great deal in such an exercise.

If your folk are resistant to the reduction of air time, use another approach. You might get your hands on a decent tape recorder (check with your station about level of quality needed). In most cases, someone in the congregation will have adequate equipment (and has never been asked to use his hobby for Christian service). Tape some post-worship raps (voice tracks) concerning the passage or topic which was the focus of the morning. Don't get into a like or dislike discussion of the sermon. Such critiques of the sermon are usually invitations for overt hostility from those who don't like the preacher, or polite partial reactions from those who don't want to offend. The preached word isn't really the center of worship. The whole Word of God should be the quest of the people of God. Your edit block can again come into play. Drop in the comments after the sermon. This gives a media representation of the theological point that the living Word of God is known when the whole people of God become vehicle for the work of the Holy Spirit. You will be amazed with the results of such a simple skill in the service of your creativity.

Some Catholic services have employed running commentaries or instructions to good effect during the broadcasting of the Liturgy. For the Protestant service on radio this would be pretty tricky, but not impossible. This technique is helpful for the specials. However, you will often be caught with a continuity problem with a weekly show. It will be easy to fall into explaining things with the same words each week.

Most radio stations are now using voice transmissions preserved on good quality audio cassette recorders. This is particularly true in presenting news. If your station doesn't mind the use of cassette recorded inserts, you are open to a lot of material gathered around the worship experience. The raps can be transferred to a reel tape and edited in at the proper places.

I am suggesting what can be done with the lowest possible investment of equipment and money. Your creativity in fleshing-out the Good News to meet real people in the world is the key factor. There are no limitations on what you can do within the givens of your situation.

What has been said about the creative editing of the worship service will also apply to any tape taken to a shut-in. It is a disgrace to take the complete service as it comes out on Sunday morning to a bedridden person. The patient doesn't want to listen to sixty or eighty minutes of other people doing things in praise and worship of God. The person who brings the service represents the community. Perhaps the edited form of the service for the shut-in could include a hymn (or two) and a section of the sermon. The Scripture could be read by the visitor. The prayer should be done by the caller and the patient. Many church people make the mistake of thinking that an electric medium (tape recorder) can take the place of a living community. It can't. The new equipment and communication networks must be used to support what man alone can do: actualize the gifts of the Spirit with brothers or sisters. I have explored the implications of the encounter between electric media and liturgy in another place (*Electric Liturgy*).

Some people feel that it is impossible to worship via media. Many pastors would agree with this assessment when they have to do the chapel-in-the-valley kind of devotional program. Rehashed sermons just don't seem to work very well in the midst of regular radio programming. Across the country the majority of the ministers and program directors I have met are unhappy with the existing devotional formats. Everyone seems to be caught in a circle of tradition from which we cannot quite break free. What may be holding us back is that we do not have a vital option. Some alternatives to this deadlock are available.

C. SPOTS BEFORE YOUR EARS

Maybe "devotional" is a good description of this form of religion on radio. Worship is usually described as the people (community) joining in praise of God. Worship is pretty hard to do through electric media.

The manager of a station in a rural community called with a problem. The daily devotional program was aired at 10:30 A.M. It featured a different clergyman from the community each day. He had just seen the rating books and realized that he lost most of his audience during this time. The listeners switched to a competitive station during the fifteen-minute program. He was worried about changing the program because most of the participating clergy would hear two or three people mention the show. This would lead them to believe that there was a huge audience. The church leaders are used to this kind of limited feedback and tend to misinterpret it. The station manager wanted to know if I would lead a workshop from which could come some new kind of devotional programming.

We decided that a good alternative to this block of religious broadcast would be a regular series of public service spots. There was a question as to whether or not the local clergymen could create regular spots. The station agreed to air fifteen one-minute spots a day for the community churches. They could be produced in the station's studio.

The group of twenty-five clergymen gathered at the station. We had a number of exercises to sensitize us to the discipline of expressing our thoughts in a terse manner which would have an impact on the listeners. Each participant had been asked to bring a recent sermon. After hearing examples of national spot material produced by the major denominations, we reworked those sermons. Groups of three clergymen dealt with the sermon material to reduce it to a manageable message. The participants were amazed how much could be cut away. As an exercise in cross reference, the Sermon on the Mount was used to illustrate how tersely the Word could be presented.

The trios analyzed the style of commercial spots, particularly the work of Stan Freberg. It seemed that he opened with a "tease" *to get attention.* He then introduced the *message* and concluded with a hook or *something clever as a way of getting out.* His spots sometimes delayed the message until interest had been built up to a desirable level. The group was surprised to see that a religious message could be delivered through the use of humor.

Each cadre was asked to take a few minutes to analyze the people of their community. After they developed the profile of their people, they shared the results with the whole group. They then returned to their units to develop a series of spots. As a stimulation, each group was given scraps of newspaper and magazine pages. These random cross sections of life were augmented by a single passage of Scripture. Sound effects and other simple production aids were made

46

available. These first generation spots were then re-corded on cassette tape recorders for class analysis.

The results were exhilarating. Everybody was pleased by the kinds of things developed in this process. The clergymen who wanted to present straight Scripture were aided in delivering this message to the audience. Dialogues, humorous skits, commentaries with sound effects, and poetry were also utilized by many to ex-press the Good News.

The station manager agreed to run fifteen of these spots a day. Each clergyman agreed to produce fif-teen to start with. The spots would be mixed and played several times a week. A production schedule was developed, and a local churchman was assigned as producer. The area now had a blanket coverage of religious input in the midst of regular programming. The impact was much more effective than the previous chapel-in-the-valley once a day. Both the clergymen and station manager were happy with this alternative style of communication.

The spot announcement is a familiar part of our lis-tening experience. It is the vehicle through which most advertising is done. Stations know this style of pro-gramming best of all. Most of the national denom-inations have followed the highly successful ex-perience of the United Presbyterian Church and now produce spots for local programming. Ed Willingham and Tom Bender have drawn together sixty of these religious spots onto a C-60 audio cassette tape. It may be obtained from the Metropolitan Detroit Council of Churches ("Spots Before Your Ears," 600 Palms Build-ing, Detroit, Michigan, 48201).

These spots are usually sent directly to the station if there is not a full-time religious broadcaster in the area. In many cases the spots get lost in the weekly inflow of public service spots. One helpful strategy would be to use the relationship you have developed with the station people to keep them informed of your church's interest in the airing of good religious spots. There is usually some announcement sent to local churches when a spot is released. Your contact with the station may make the difference in whether or not the spot will be aired. It is a good practice to respond warmly to a station when they do run some of this nationally produced material. Stations usually only get complaints and are particularly appreciative of positive responses.

D. PACKAGED RELIGIOUS SHOWS

In just about every kind of religious program area there are taped packaged shows available from different denominations. There are a number of fine quality worship and devotional shows offered without cost to the local station. Your market area probably has a number of these shows on the air. They are usually scheduled in very bad time slots, often being aired at an early hour in the Sunday morning ghetto. You can get more information about these shows from your denomination or by contacting Lois Anderson at the Broadcast and Film Commission, (475 Riverside Drive, New York, New York, 10027). This office acts as distributor for the mass media material produced by the major church bodies.

It is quite tempting to recommend some of this well-produced material to your local stations. However, you may not find much enthusiasm for your offering. A station would rather have locally produced material. The programming which originates from the community is more in keeping with the aims of the station. The broadcaster is there to serve your community. It also helps if he can show such local efforts at license renewal time.

A station may even favor the typical Sunday morning worship service to the nationally produced spots or packaged programs because churches are willing to buy time. In spite of the churches' good intentions in paying their way, I am against the buying of local time in most cases. As I stated earlier, the airwaves belong to your community. If the programming is good, it should be of interest to at least a segment of the audience. Free time is there if you deserve it. It is so much easier for most churches to gather money for the Sunday morning broadcast than to do creative public service programming. However, this step locks your church and the whole religious community into a procedure which will make effective mass media evangelism impossible. You owe it to the stations and to those outside the church to help forge a style of public service broadcasting which can change the lives of people. Most stations are not simply money-hungry businesses. They are composed of people who care about their community. Of course, the business aspect of the broadcasting is important. However, the fifteen dollars to forty dollars you pay for that service will not make or break a station. Buying time can create a mentality which will cripple the thrust of the religious community's ministry via mass media. In some major markets, stations pride themselves on not taking paid religious shows.

Get a tape of the "Protestant Hour" (through the Broadcast and Film Commission, see p. 48) or some other good worship program. It will be helpful in terms of your own planning and work. The nationally produced spots will also be a real help to your stations and to the thinking of your media ministry planners. However, the final battle to present a message of hope and love via mass media must come from the local folk. Nothing can replace *you*. You are the only person who can respond to the call to minister in your area. No one can know your people in the same way you do.

In some areas there will be a religious broadcaster or council broadcaster. He or she will probably work for an ecumenical group as a full- or part-time person serving in the area of mass media. These are good folk. However, don't be hesitant in your media concern just because an expert is around. In fact, the presence of such a special ministry will aid your people in doing something about mass media. The expert will be able to help you reach stations or focus on a particular aspect of such a ministry. He can also give you easy access to the packaged shows produced for national distribution. The council broadcaster also needs your help in doing this important work.

There is another dimension to mass media and the syndicated show which must be mentioned in passing. We tend to forget that there must be some way of connecting the human and the electric environment. A broadcast may work out just as we had planned. However, did it really touch anyone? What kind of long-range change did it bring? Does the person retain the Good News we have been able to flesh-out as he watches the next eight commercials and the following show? The religious show has been excellent. So what? It must touch and move people with the Good News before we can call it theological communication.

A number of mass media people in local churches

are creating courses which use taped religious and commercial programs in study groups. This kind of study of media programming may help the religious person to carry his theology back into the electric marketplace. I fear that people often turn off their theological sensors when they sit down for an evening of listening and watching. This is not to say that the Christian faith should take the fun out of entertainment. It should just put more meaning into it. There are a number of radio series which are ideal for such off-the-air local study. Some people have media and theology courses which utilize all kinds of mass media programming for study. One church used the audio tracks from "All in the Family" for a theological study. Serious study of such programs can help sensitize Christians to theological issues in what they thought were purely secular programs.

E. YOUTH PROGRAMS

One of the hottest areas of media interest is the so-called youth market. Most stations want this audience. This sector of the society has money to spend. And, as is obvious, it is closely related to modern music. Most radio stations program around music. The message is that the audience' love of music can be translated into a strong sales factor. In other words, the price you pay for the music and radio personalities you enjoy is buying the products they advertise. It is interesting that one of the major concerns of the church is also youth. People in just about every religious tradition I have encountered are worried about the loss of their young people. The gap between young people on the church roll and ones who actually participate in the local program is startling. They just aren't around anymore. A number of extra-church groups have been flourishing in recent years. They have been picking up these drop-out kids without much trouble. It is not our task here to explore the many reasons behind this situation. However, for our purposes it is necessary to understand that both the church and the popular radio station want to touch young people. This identity of interest comes from different sources, but the interest is still the same. This means that there is an excellent opportunity for ministry in media to this age group.

1. *Packaged Shows*

There are several models of programming from which you can choose. The area of packaged shows offers a number of excellent choices. "Powerline" (Southern Baptist) and "Silhouette" (American Lutheran) are just two of the programs which have been well received by stations and audiences. "Powerline" combines music and soft religious rap by an adult host. The pace is fast and fits into most top-forty formats. "Silhouette" is another rap and music format. The discussion comes from church youth across the country. The pace is again contemporary and interesting. "What's It All About" (Presbyterian Church in U.S.) is in a spot form of three- to four-minute's length. A top song is played, and in the context of the song a brief interview with the performer is conducted by Bill Huie. These programs are free of charge to local stations. Your help might be needed to get them on the air in a good time slot. Again, consult the Broadcasting and Film Commission for further information on available packaged programs.

2. "The Place": Music and Rap

"The Place" is a concept originated in Pittsburgh on KQV. It is now being produced locally in almost two hundred markets. The format is quite simple. An adult host and a group of teens rap in the context of the music played on the local station. The raps are fairly short, and three to five songs are used in a typical thirty-minute program. It combines the strengths of "Silhouette" with the advantage of being a local production. On some stations "The Place" is taped. It can also be done live.

The host is a key part of the concept. He must be a facilitator who can provide a sustaining support for the young people who produce the show each week. This is not a format for those who want to lead young people into talking about church things. In my four years with the show, I found that we usually ended up talking about theology as a result of our free rap. When we got to this juncture of sharing, it was on the guests' turf, and it was real. I often welcomed young people off the streets to be part of the show. The exchange was always religious and fresh. I even used students to do the taping and editing. We had our own production studio and would deliver the final tape to the station for airing.

It is quite striking what 15-, 16-, and 17-year-old men and women can do when given this kind of opportunity. We used to produce the opening after we had done the show. How could we grab the audience with a powerful sound experience which summarizes what we had been talking about? On occasion the voice of Hitler and the bombing of London came cracking across the opening seconds of the show. The inter-mix of two versions of the same tune sometimes graced the show. The content would depend on the creativity of the young people producing that particular show. The hosts who have had the best luck with this youth format are those who have created the environment in which honest probing of feelings and issues can take place. I often used a lot of inductive questions to get into a person's life in the context of his music.

The United Methodist Church, through its radio and television arm (TRAFCO), enables local folk to get training to produce the show in their area. William Richards and Richard Dohrmann will be glad to aid you in this task (1525 McGavock St. Nashville, Tennessee, 37203).

The nice thing about this concept is that it involves young people in doing a media ministry. It also enables the church to meet this audience in terms of its idiom. Almost any kind of music station can cater to this kind of format. Local churches have also used the show to get discussions going in their high school church school classes. This can reinforce the bridge between the mass media and the local group which seems so important in our age.

3. *Sound Collage: "Open Door"*

Another model for youth programming is well reflected in the work of Bud Frimoth and the God-Squad Youth in Portland, Oregon. They produce a weekly show for KGW called, "Open Door." The production team created thematic shows in the style of a sound collage. Music, poetry, raps, and sound intermix to create good radio that touches people. This is a good example of a show which creates a good preevangelism environment. A typical script written by the young people is as follows:

"Open Door"   (#70)   *Theme: Adolescence*

Teaser: Record — Howdy Doody — Welcome to Howdy Doody

Voice 1: I'm a man, now!

Voice 2: You're just a boy.

1: They'll trust me more!

2: You're just a kid.

1: I'll be someone now!

2: You don't even have a job.

1: But I'm growing up—you've got to let me go.

2: Listen to me, son. You're in that stage of life called "adolescence." I know how you feel. You see, when I was a boy about your age, I had mixed feelings, too! But I learned to handle them. I worked hard to come up to where I am now. My parents (*talk over, T.O.*) were hard on me and I knew it, but I (*fade voice*) understand now why they did it. I overcame those feelings and turned out to be a man. . . . (Just hang in there, boy. Someday you'll understand too . . .)

(0:29) *Theme*

Voice 1: Adolescence, the second big shock to the human body after birth and early childhood, that's what we want to explore today on "Open Door."

Voice 2: Sometimes, amid all the confusion of growing up, facts get twisted around a little. Rumors are usually stereotyped for gossiping housewives at coffee breaks, but listen to this next conversation between some teen-agers.

Steve: Hey, Jane! Wait a minute . . .

Jane: What's up?

Steve: Did you hear about Alice?

Jane: No. What?! What?! What?!

Steve: It's only a rumor but I heard . . .

Jane: Yes?

Steve: I heard that Alice actually talked to that new guy, Jim.

Jane: You're kidding! Where were they?

Steve: I don't know. That's all I could get out of Sue. But she's Alice's best friend, so you can bet it's the unquestionable truth!

Jane: Thanks. See ya! . . . Hey Mark, did you hear about Alice and Jim?

Mark: No!

Jane: Alice and Jim were caught kissing in the locker well. And both of them were taken to the office.

Mark: Really? Well, I'll see you later. I've got a class . . . Dave, did you catch the news about Alice and Jim?

Dave: No, I haven't heard a thing!

Mark: Well, Alice and Jim were taken to the principal's office. And from what I've heard Alice is pregnant!

Dave:	Wow! How did I ever miss out on this? Catch you later. . . . Wait a minute, George! Did ya hear about Jim and Alice? Alice is pregnant and the baby is due any day now.
George:	Boy, you sure are slow!
Dave:	Why?
George:	I just heard that Jim has left school and Alice moved to Texas and had twins.
Dave:	Gee, no one ever tells me anything!

(2:31)	*Music*	"There's a World"—Neil Young—(3:00/09)
(5:31)	*Voice:*	Dear Sir:

Thank you for the excellent essay "On Being an American Parent." Oh, how I wish every parent and future parent would read it and take it to heart!

I love my parents and I know they love me, but they've ruined my life. . . . I could never tell my parents anything! It was always "I'm too busy . . . too tired . . . can't you think of better things . . . oh your friends are wrong . . . they're stupid." As a result I stopped telling my parents anything. All communications ceased. We never had that very important thing—fun.

Oh, we had love. Prompted on my side by an ever-present fear of my mother and pity for my father, and prompted on their side by the thought that I was their responsibility and if I went wrong, they would be punished by God.

After four rotten years in a . . . girl's school (I did have two or three wonderful teachers), I'm now stuck in an even worse . . . women's college. Only the best for me! They knew I didn't want to come but made me anyhow. Their daughter wasn't going to be corrupted! I had already been saved from the evils of early dating and doing things that "everybody else" did. What is the result of this excellent upbringing? I'm eighteen years old, drink whenever I get the chance, have smoked pot, and as of a very eventful Thanksgiving vacation, am no longer a virgin. Why? Was it my parents or just me? I'm so very confused—but who can I talk to? Not my parents. My parents could read this and never dream it was their daughter. I have only one important plea to parents . . . Listen, listen, and listen again. Please, I know the consequences, and I'm in hell.

(7:31)	*Music*	*"She's Leaving Home"*—Beatles— (3:24/05) (*with T.O. at very end of song*)
	Voice:	Maybe listening is the most important part of loving. Please! Let me listen while there's still time before the kids start leaving home.
(10:55)	*Voice 1:*	"Who are you?"
	Voice 2:	"I?—I hardly know, sir, just at present—at least I know who I *was* when I got up this morning, but I think I must have been changed several times since then."
	1:	"What do you mean by that? Explain yourself!"
	2:	"I can't explain *myself*. I'm afraid, sir, because I'm not myself, you see."
	Voice 1:	"No, I don't see."
(11:20)	*Music:*	"Eighteen"—Alice Cooper— (3:00)
(14:20)	*Music:*	"White Bird"—It's a Beautiful Day—(6:06) (*Bring up song over the end of "Eighteen" and immediately start T.O.*)
	Voice:	What makes me the way I am? Why do I do the things I do? Am I for real? Am I really here? I feel so trapped—so caged in— let me go! I don't understand. I just don't understand.

(20:26) *Music:* "La Chanson de Claudine"—Mason Williams—(4:08)

Voice: (*T.O.*) I had always heard about teenage troubles . . . (*ends*) Sometimes it's hard to see with tears in your eyes. (*Bring up music till the end of the song.*)

Voice 1: I'm a man, now!

2: You're just a boy.

1: They'll trust me more.

2: You're just a kid.

1: I'll be someone now.

2: You don't even have a job.

1: But I'm growing up—you've got to let me go.

2: Listen to me, son. You're in that stage called adolescence. I know how you feel. You see, when I was a boy about your age . . .

1: No, I've listened to you for years. Now, please, listen to me. I *want* to grow up. I *have* to grow up. I *need* to grow up. I'm not a kid anymore, and I'm not a grown man, but I'm trying to grow up, Dad. I'm trying. What else can I do but try to be me? I'm your son, and I'll always be your son, but sons grow up and leave home and make new homes for themselves. And then those same sons get married and have sons of their own, who grow up and at one point in their life, they leave, too. That's the way it is, Dad.

Voice 1:	Dad, I love you for bringing me into existence, and I'll love you now, for letting me exist—as me.
(25:44) *Music:*	"Crossroads"—Don McClean—(3:34) (*T.O. after first two beats*)
Voice:	"I have promises to keep And miles to go before I sleep And miles to go before I sleep."
(29:18) *Bud:*	Do you remember that Jesus was a teen-ager, too? And on at least one occasion we know, he faced a generation gap with his parents. It could be he understands adolescence, too! If you want to rap a bit, why not call me? I'm Bud, my number is 292-2448. That's 292-2448. If you don't get through to me or to one of the God-Squaders, the first time, do keep trying. Material was put together by God-Squaders, Margaret, with original material by Kelly, two anonymous students, plus authors Lewis Carroll and Robert Frost. "Open Door" is the youthful contribution to the Interfaith Broadcasting Commission and the Greater Portland Council of Churches. I'm your host, Bud Frimoth, saying bye-bye for just now.

This script is a good example of the kind of preparation that must go into a production of this nature. You will be amazed at the high level youth work this kind of project can create. The actual style of the outline preparation will depend on the form used by your local station. One important thing in scripting is arranging it so the engineer at the station understands what will happen. A script is a means of communication among the participants in the project. Whatever facilitates this understanding is a good script form.

The value of having student-listeners originate the programming is that you will be able to cover a wide spectrum of concerns and ideas. One adult producer cannot be as creative alone as he can in a community. The adult plays an important role in these local concepts. A station is often worried about continuity in its programming. Anyone off the street can come up with one show, but it is creative staying power that a radio station must consider. Most adults have experienced youth projects which were not carried to their conclusion. This is why most mass media folk will be quite skeptical about young people doing their own shows. The adult involvement will usually assure the station that the series will be maintained.

Note that Bud Frimoth (9100 S. W. Wilshire, Portland, Oregon, 97225) also encourages the audience to call him off the air. This extension of personal follow-up of the mass media input is very important. We must be willing to complete that which our message has stimulated. This is often one of the real shortcomings of mass media. Commercial producers are mainly concerned with getting the show done and seeing that viewers buy the product advertised. The Christian has the theological commitment to go the second and third miles of media extension to complete the ministry of Christ. We are not limited to only the outer man or our neighbor at a distance. The Good News is to be made incarnate through our lives and shared with the household of faith and with those who are far off.

4. *Jesus Music: "A Joyful Noise"*

Another interesting youth format is that developed by Frank M. Edmondson, Jr., "A Joyful Noise." It is a low profile religious show which features Jesus music. It is a local show which is now aired in five different markets. The hour format is quite well adapted to the young adult audience. The line of crossover is quite subtle and very important in terms to what you are trying to communicate to your audience. Frank is a radio professional who has developed a print-support extension of the show's format. *Rock Is Jesus* is a magazine devoted entirely to Jesus Music (Box 13504, Wichita, Kansas, 67213). He is attempting to explore an important phenomenon in contemporary music as an extension of his theological concern.

5. *Talk-Phone Shows: "Rap Around"*

One of the most popular formats in the past couple years has been called the talk-phone program. In a few cities you may find a station devoting its whole programming to this style of radio. In most major markets just about every station has such a talk show. In some cases the host takes calls as they come in. Most stations have some kind of phone producer who screens or intercepts the calls to ready the folk for being on the air. This latter approach seems to be the best for several reasons. It gives the caller a chance to be reminded about the ten-second tape delay used by most stations. The phone producer can also help the caller focus his comment or question. Thirdly, the producer can easily keep a log of the subject matter which was raised by the call. This flow sheet will help the host evaluate the show's development and drift. The written log or summary of the calls will also help the station at license renewal time to present the range of community concerns treated by the licensee.

The host plays an important role in the direction of the show. There have been some shows where teens talk to a clergyman. This format usually deals with religious questions, and with the right panelists, this concept can work quite well. The adults are the resource persons for ethical and religious content questions. Other hosts tend to take no position on questions. They act as a reflector for the caller. It is their conception of their role to draw the caller out and thereby help him clarify what he thinks. In most cities you will find a talk show host who wants to create controversy and exitement. He will attack just about every caller. It is his role to challenge everyone.

A good way to think through the process of developing a youth phone show is to review the evolution of "Rap Around." I first hosted this show in September of 1970. It is still on the air. It was our original concept to stimulate the audience to bring to us the issues which bothered them. Audio stimuli were dropped into the first two shows to get a reaction from the audience. For example, I might play Al Capp's burning assessment of demonstrators. As the host, it was our style to deal with the discussions on a feeling level. For instance, a student called and stated that he did not like the columnist, Al Capp. He wished that we would get rid of him. My response was to encourage a bit of fantasy. "If I entrusted him to you for two weeks, how would you regroove him?" We then spent ten minutes working through his fantasy and trying to decide what could and what could not be changed by our action.

A student called during the first show and proclaimed that I was a "homo." I didn't cut him off. The next Sunday evening (9:00-11:00) he called again and said that I was "queer." The third week he called and asked what I thought about obscene callers. I went into a rap about how I thought that people shouldn't treat the obscene caller with anger and hatred. He just needed love and understanding. The caller hesitated and then said, "I need love too." He had been able to experience the transition from shouting for attention to a relationship where we could talk. He was accepted.

It must have been the fourth or fifth week when a fourteen-year-old girl called and confessed that she was pregnant. Her guy had left town, and she felt that she could not tell her parents. We talked for fifteen minutes or so. She promised to call me off the air. The next year and a half of the show featured only people who called in with problems. At no time did I suggest that people should share the private aspect of their lives. I don't think that counseling can be done on the radio. However, a precounseling environment can be reinforced through the personal medium of radio. People can experience the satisfaction of talking with someone and learning that it is good to attempt a human relationship.

I try to manifest my Christian faith by the way that I handle the show. How can I incarnate the love of Christ in such a way that the audience can feel what a relationship in Jesus is like? For one thing, it means that every problem has to be handled with the same degree of care and concern. The thirteen-year-old girl who has just lost her best girlfriend is treated with the same patience as the woman who calls about her family tragedy. "My husband killed our baby by accident.

He buried it himself in the cemetery. The police found out and put him in jail. I had a little nervous breakdown. My husband hasn't written in two years. I lost custody of the children. I want my husband and children back. What can I do?" These two people have very different levels of concern. However, on "Rap Around" I try to care for them with the same depth.

The response to this new drift in the show was startling. Our mail climbed to one hundred letters a week. An audience rating at the time indicated that we had 73 percent of the teen and preteen audience. In 1971 we received the Golden Mike Award "for Pennsylvania's best local radio program in the interest of youth." It was presented to us by the American Legion Auxiliary.

The letters were quite striking. It seems that the linkage of the medium of radio with print (letters) is a good combination. People would write twenty-five-page letters to explain their problems. The satisfaction of getting a letter, enhanced by the power of the music medium on this number one rock station (KQV), is enormous. The letters came from a number of strange sources. There were a lot of epistles from young teens and preteens concerning basic problems of coping with life (dating, family relationships, etc.). However, we also received notes and letters from young adults, parents, and grandparents. Apparently some families listen together. One nurse wrote to say that she appreciated the fact that a person called about the fear of having venereal disease. She had wanted to talk with her eleven- and thirteen-year-old children about VD, but hadn't wanted to introduce the topic unnaturally. They always listen to "Rap Around" on the way back from their Sunday visit to their grandmother's house. After the call on VD, they had talked about this area of concern as a family.

Letters came from the children of local political officials asking for help with difficulties in their family life. A famous criminal who had been sentenced to the electric chair wrote from solitary confinement. A housewife in a wealthy suburb wrote to offer aid to a pregnant girl who had called. She confessed that she had been in the same situation ten years earlier. A number of letters came from retardees. Addicts, homosexuals, and other subculture folk also wrote to "Rap Around."

When a person called in with a religious question or to share a religious experience he had just had, this would be explored in full. The audience was told that I am a Presbyterian minister if someone raised that question. However, I was "Dennis" to most callers. We tried to support people who were groping for direction and understanding. Several young people would write as many as three letters a week when they had nowhere else to turn. One young girl was trapped in a family situation which she felt was unbearable. There was no support for her in her particular rural context. The letters to "Rap Around" were her escape valve. I would respond with one letter to her three or four. She just needed a window of hope and care.

It was also satisfying to get what I call "second generation" letters. These epistles indicated a transition from crisis to hope. The linear part of our communication often contained a celebration of improvement in an emotional situation. One girl had become pregnant, and her mother had forced her to go to New York for an abortion. A cycle of distrust and resentment entered into their relationship. It was delightful to receive her letter about six months after the abortion.

"The sun is shining. I have finally been able to do what you and my conscience were urging me to do. Mother and I sat down and started talking about the whole situation. There was some anger and more tears. However, we embraced and felt so close after the two hours. This all happened about three weeks ago. Things are so much better now. Thanks for being there when I needed someone. The sun is shining now."

Much of the show's reaction came from those who seemed to need a male figure with whom they could relate. Our society has created an image of the male as hard and unfeeling. Perhaps the feminists are reminding us that the fully human male is a feeling and caring person also. A number of young working women wrote about affairs in which they had become entangled with bosses and fellow workers, who were married. "I have talked with my girlfriends about this. It is just like talking to myself. I can't talk to my dad. He would kill me. I trust you. You are a man and perhaps you can give me another perspective on this whole thing." It is amazing to note that most mass media helpers or counselors are women. There is a need for the church to enable the image of the caring male to emerge.

I have a mental goal of doing, in a different context and with a different focus, what Fred Rogers does with children. This creative United Presbyterian minister provides creative energy which manifests itself as "Misterogers Neighborhood" on hundreds of stations across the country. He provides a ministry of care and love to each child, and he does this theological work without using the familiar religious language of the church. For most of us, it is ego-gratifying to "say" the words of salvation to a person. It makes us feel complete. We can rest assured that we have fulfilled our commitment to preach because we have said the words which mean something to us. However, I feel that in the electric age, Christ calls forth messengers who are prepared to sacrifice this ego satisfaction if necessary. The kind of mass media evangelism we are suggesting may mean that you will not fully realize the fruits of your ministry. You will be sowing love, which is based on your commitment to Jesus Christ, in order that others may harvest. This "missionary" understanding of evangelism has often been lacking in our outreach. We have failed to grasp the hope which is based on other than the tangible measures of failure or success. The upward curve of the sales chart is satisfying and we should thank God when we have these highs. However, the extension of faith in evangelism cannot be based on such an evaluation of our ministry.

This model of radio ministry can be very frustrating. Despair is just around the corner when you are doing media in the electric marketplace. There is always the possibility that you are not really listening to what your audience is saying. Perhaps you do not flesh-out the love of God in Jesus Christ for them. This kind of ministry demands a tough theological stance. I personally believe that those commissioned (and the local church should develop occasions for calling people to special local ministries in the context of celebration) to this work must draw upon the continuous study of Scripture. I have spent extensive time on this key discipline in the SOS (Switched on Scripture) and RAP series of enabling audio cassettes (Abingdon Audio•Graphics). The process of biblical exegesis (digging out the meaning) not only releases the message of Scripture, but also develops a creative mind-set, which enables the believer to dig into the so-called secular life for the work of salvation. This theologically rugged style of media work is demanding and very freeing. It releases the Christian to work in the context of music, people, and films without having to impose upon them the language of another realm.

It is very important that the local church provide the support of the community for this kind of outreach. The lonely media proclamation must rise out of the community in order to be creative and authentically of the Spirit. So many ministries of local laymen and clergy get chopped down at this point. The fact that the Berrigan brothers could bring along the Society of Jesus in their ministry made their thought and action have an authenticity and depth which would have been missed otherwise. So much social action or evangelistic activity is meaningless for Christians when it just represents doing its own thing and doesn't speak out of the community. One can easily get lost in a lone social or spiritual ministry without the guiding role of the theological community of brothers and sisters.

The electric media mix is very seductive. The medium can easily erode the message and the messenger. This has been true in any age. It is man's risk whenever he attempts to flesh-out the Word of God. As soon as our eyes catch the words on a page of Scripture, we have made an interpretation which has been colored by our immediate and total history. However, our faith commitment enables us to take this risk. The threat of distorting and misunderstanding faith is one way of defining life. To live is to risk error. In our charged environment the risks just seem more explosive and more difficult. Isolation is our enemy. The diverse body held together by one Lord is the key to authentic outreach.

This kind of reasoning is dangerous. If we do touch the lives of people with our witness of the Good News, what will they find in the support community? It is to our shame that those enamored of Christ come to us for nurture and leave hungry. As one young person told me at the end of a dry and nonparticipatory communion service, "I was promised the Body and Blood of Christ. All they gave me was fish food."

Radio has the particular power to stimulate and tease the possibility of trust and intimacy. It is important that we link this kind of spiritual foreplay with an actualized community. Our calling is such that we cannot just be another hype for things which will eventually disappoint. We must deliver the goods in the theological sense made so real by this style of using mass media. So many of the "Rap Around" letters begin, "You will probably not answer this letter. I have written help columns before, and they only sent back a mimeographed sheet asking me to buy their book." It is also significant that many of the writers will begin their second letter to me, "I was surprised to receive your letter. I guess that you do care. Now here is my real problem."

"Rap Around" is an interesting case study. It is a concept in constant change. There have been a number of shifts in its direction during the past two years. During the heavy problem period of time, some interesting mind-wine was sampled. My analysis of our early response and acceptance was formed around my understanding of mass media and radio in particular. The show was aired at the end of the station's top music program. Marshall McLuhan has suggested that radio is actually a tribal drum by which certain segments of the community can keep in touch. The young person can turn up the radio and clear the room of those who do not move to the same rhythm as he does. Even though the teen-ager is sitting alone listening to his favorite station while he does his homework, he knows that others are tuned into his source of vibrations. This sense of community and identity is usually utilized to sell products to the listener. The disc jockey is the priest who administers the vehicle (music) of community. He also sells the goods advertised on the station.

My genuine appreciation for the other air personalities on KQV has meant that they kindly accepted me into this magic web of media priesthood. They kid me about the show and provide regular promotion for what is coming up on my show later. This gives me and "Rap Around" a sense of belonging to this pantheon of media power. Instead of using this power associated with music to sell things, I try to support people with care as they struggle with their humanity. This gives me a power leverage far surpassing that which my personhood or qualifications deserve. So it is with everyone in media. The personalities pick up influence and roles transcending their abilities and personalities.

This is a kind of advantage that the church has been slow to understand and use theologically. Most of the affirmation given to church folk in local roles tends to feed the ego but less obviously becomes power to facilitate the spiritual quest of the community. This kind of power always exists in deep relationships. The love for that favorite teacher should become the power factor which enables a young student to get grasped by an academic discipline and the love of learning. However, mass media can create such power more quickly and to a greater extent. It is rarely used to aid man in his quest to reinforce his humanity. I am suggesting that this may be one of the most important contributions the Christian faith has to make in the context of these new power dimensions to human life. It is the Christian who can, in the context of community, overcome the selfish use of power and direct that energy back into the massmediaman. The stars of radio and television sometimes have a difficult time with this channeling of energy. It often destroys them and/or lets them use it on the audience in a destructive manner.

One brainstorm which would rechannel the "Rap Around" energy back into the listeners is a concept I call the "Electric Ombudsman." It seems that we have become a broker between human need and human resources. It is jolting to face the reality that in our modern communication complex, educated people still do not know how to get from their personal, emotional, and spiritual needs to the sources of aid. They need a human mediator to make this linkage. It suddenly dawned on me that this just might be the new role for the radio station in the 70s and 80s.

In the past, stations have fulfilled their public responsibility by doing specials on problems (informing the listeners of issues), programming the audience's interests (formats), and taking editorial stands (ethical positions). However, the real power of these stations resided in the electronic umbrella of community it sustains. A station could be the bridge between human needs and human resources! On the air we could provide a model of what could happen when a person reaches out for help. Short, one-minute excerpts from "Rap Around" conversations could be dropped into the regular format. The jock on the air could suggest that anyone was free to call Dennis at that time. A person calling at that moment would probably reach someone else who was manning the phones. This trained person would introduce himself as one of my friends. The caller could share a particular problem. Behind the people handling the phones would be a computer bank of information. If a person called to say, for example, that she was pregnant, Catholic, sixteen years old, and from a particular part of the city, the kind of help she needs is pinpointed to a large degree. The computer could provide the information most accurately. Of course, the fact that a computer has been used for this information retrieval need not be mentioned. The "Rap Around" person would maintain the high level of personal care.

This model is not totally new. And, of course, it has not yet become a reality. However, the factors needed to make it work exist in most major marketing areas: resource people, teen talk shows, and hotlines. The new part of this proposal involves the *interlinking* of these existing components into a new totality. This is the factor which seems to have been missing in so many of our attempts to reach the needs of people. The failure to bring together the existing fragments of power into a central resource bank is perhaps the greatest weakness in our struggle to be a caring society and church. This is not to suggest that new conglomerates are the answer. I think that new communication power chains can be accomplished without falling prey to the dangers of megastructuring. In fact, I think that, far from being threatened by centralization, we are in a period of swift and radical disintegration of the American society on just about every level. The church is the best example of the breakdown of the centralized approach. The mind-set at the time when COCU was first proposed and our current state of thinking is radically different.

There is much in our theology which would suggest special ministries in our mass media society. We affirm that Christ has put it all together. While our faith brings a totally new understanding of the fragmentation of human life, we have not been robbed of our uniqueness. Yet, American society is in danger of falling back into individualism, which can only heighten loneliness and fragmentation. The Christian does not claim individuality as his essence. The life, death, and resurrection of Christ has created a total person. There is a freshness and a never-beforeness to this new man in Christ. However, his uniqueness is found in the community. The biblical record of those first incorporated into the body of Christ provides a rich witness to this process. The New Testament figures break through as real persons. We discern their unique personhood as they undertake the process of becoming in Christ. However, the individual partakers of God's gift in Christ make up a totality which is more than the various parts.

The "Electric Ombudsman" is a concept which could interrelate existing power structures in such a way that people would end up where they needed to be. In most urban communities the components for such a model now exist. There are enough self-interest factors to bring together these resources for the program. A company just might be willing to loan the use of a computer and thereby get a tax write-off. The station could demonstrate beyond a question to the FCC that it was indeed serving the community through this concept. This approach would also draw many listeners. The social agencies and church service people are very willing to gain a better access to those in need. I also believe that these power units in our society do care about people and will respond to a concept that aims at serving their best interests. Well, this idea is just a dream at this point. It is a possibility which "Rap Around" did not realize for a number of reasons. However, this model could be a reality in any large community. And I, personally, would be glad to help any interested person all I could. Just call me and see.

After about a year of our show, I became restless with limited concerns expressed by the calls. How could we probe some new corners of existence? I hadn't used any taped inserts after the first two or three shows. We were caught in a bind because the callers phoned us with their particular problem in hand and so many calls were backed up to go on the air that there was little cross talk between callers. Some persons would call thirty or forty minutes before air time and wait on hold in order to get on the show. I started wondering what a cassette tape recorder furnished by the news department of the station could do. I could rap with hitchhikers, female gas station attendants, a retired coal miner, the returning soldier. Minidocumentaries were built out of this kind of rap. Engineer John Yurek would dub the statements that I wanted from the person being interviewed from cassette to open reel. We would put these on cartridges. I would select some appropriate music for the background. For the first seven or ten minutes I would use a radio news style of combining the cartridges with my live questions and background comments. This gave the segment a live quality. I was trying to bring into the discussion persons who could or would not call us. These folk were a part of our community who could be present in a way that the phones did not permit.

I also added movie reviews at the half-hour. I tried to extend my concept of dealing with art and life on a feeling level. Technical aspects of a film were not important to the listener. How could I extract a feature of humanity from a bit of entertainment art? I would even review X- and R-rated films. It was my contention that often the controversy over a film could do more damage than the actual viewing of it. For instance, a lot of young people were not able to see *Easy Rider* when it was playing across the country a few years ago. The rumors passed around by the young people I knew misrepresented the actual film. They had heard about what a groovy life these guys were living with their bikes and grass. They also heard about some terrible adults who shot the good guys at the film conclusion. Of course, this is not the message one gets from seeing the film. In a real sense, the heroes did not emerge as heroes. One is left with their sense of despair and confusion. The bad guys are not very adult. I wish that the "Captain America" crowd who could not get in to see the film had actually experienced it. Without endorsing a controversial film I try to develop a process of probing the artists, expressions of life for deeper and important clues to our humanity. The reviews are often produced with the sound track music in the background.

It may have been my own interest in music and its superstars which led me to an important transition in the show. Bob Harper, the operations manager of KQV, helped me gain access to the performers passing through Pittsburgh. My first interviews were pretty shaky. I soon learned not to talk to a band as a group. You have to get them one at a time, or they tend to play the cute news conference role of early Beatles. Alone the members of a group will be deep and personal. The British road bands are particularly open. I also learned that most of these rock stars are not interviewed by the electric media. There will be an occa-sional film or TV special. Articles in print appear re-gularly in rock magazines like *Rolling Stone*. However, a star cuts himself off from the emotional demands of his audience, and there is little personal contact to fill the gap between himself and his audience.

The early interviews tried to open the whole realm of the music and mass media world. I talked with pro-moters, roadies, fans, ushers, and policemen. Everyone was open and sharing. There was a ministry to these folk in just treating them as persons. I tried to draw them out concerning their life-style. I remember a long rap with Edgar Winter. His group White Trash had just torn up the crowd with a fantastic set. We were in his dressing room. This young albino from Texas sat on the grubby couch with a striking woman next to him. I sat on the floor in front of him operating my cassette recorder. His rap was warm and free. He seemed to be unwinding after his intense performance. I mentioned that we were really knocked out by his set. "It was bad. My voice . . . I don't know what is wrong. I used to sing every night for hours. I just can't do it anymore." He talked about the role Gospel music played in his musical development. He still liked the down-home music of his roots. We rapped about his schooling and how hard it had been for a person near-ly blind to get turned on in school. It was a good and real evening which could be shared with the "Rap A-round" folk who could never talk with him.

A strange thing began to happen as these mini-documentaries became a regular feature of the show. The first time I realized what was happening was when I interviewed David Cassidy and the Osmond Brothers at the height of their popularity. The mail grew enor-mously. I began to realize that the listeners were mythmakers. It wasn't just the fact that show business created stars. These young people wanted demigods through which to seek themselves. I interviewed one girl at the Cassidy concert and asked her why she liked the reigning star. "I like the television show he is on." This was hard for me to understand. It seemed too simple to be real. "That family is really together. They are not at all like my family. My father comes home drunk. Keith and his family like to do things together because they like each other." From nonreality this girl spins the model for what a family should be. This was her stronghold, her faith in an option to what she was experiencing at home.

Perhaps one could work through the needs and strengths of people by probing the new myths we create. The church has only touched this realm of de-mythologizing in controversial discussions of biblical stories. There is much more to this whole discussion in terms of mass media. We should also move carefully in taking away the myths that people create. What kind of solid theological substance can replace the dead myth? The church has been creating modern myths or fantasy traditions of its own. Many things that have been supported in very traditional looking contexts are in fact, new myths. What is the substance of faith, and what is nonessential? These are difficult questions. The faith community is caught in this web of human need and human fantasy as much as the massmediaman. After all, sometimes we are both.

"Rap Around" is changing again. A study of our primary audience indicated that we had all the younger teens we could ever get. However, the continuous recital of their problems turned off the young adult and perhaps didn't challenge the young listener. The station's reach was for the contemporary listener. "Rap

Around's" airing of younger problems tended to mislead the older listener about the thrust of the station.
The exploration of media art forms (music, film, TV,
etc.) through the medium of sound suggested a way
by which we might reach in two directions toward our
audience. I am now expanding the on-the-scene interviews and introducing other human extensions. If
this is where he processes and sorts himself out in the
quest for identity, perhaps real self awareness can be
found in this context. In a sense this is a deepening of
the linear language or talk forms I had used in the
first days of the show. I now have the freedom to explore the intermix of sound, human terror, and human
hope. The freeing thing about radio is that any sound
in the universe that can be captured, can be used. You
are limited only by your imagination and the company
you keep.

It is with great excitement that I try to plunge more
deeply into the changing edge of "Rap Around." Of
course, there will be callers and problems. However,
I will use selective windows for them in the format.
My phone producer Brother Patrick and I actually take
more calls off the air than ever before. I will handle
many of the coping problems through letters, also off
the air. Key situations will be aired in the talk windows.
The show will be paced faster, and when I'm interviewing a particular rock star I will use his music as the
context for the interview.

During the early format of "Rap Around," I usually
spent fifteen hours a week in preparation for the show.
The recent changes have pushed the preparation
time for the two hours of air time each Sunday to
thirty hours. With the limitation of the on-the-air calls,
the mail will increase. This is very time-consuming.
KQV has not dodged its responsibility. I am supported

by regular secretarial help to get all the mail answered within an eight- or ten-day period. The production aspects of the show will take more time and creativity. I will now be able to extend my initial explorations in the use of sound for the multimedia shows. I am anxious to explore the use of humor in serious contexts.

This model has been treated at some length in order to give you a mini-view of the kind of massaging that goes on in the process of giving form to a message on the medium of radio. The comments I made earlier about a station's sensitivity to an audience are borne out by my experience. Every strong station will pinpoint an audience it desires to reach and try to meet this audience where it can be met. This means that this medium is fluid and thrives on change. Stations can make mistakes. This usually results in someone's being fired.

I am envious of the freedom that a station has, compared to most local churches. We simply don't know our audience. While we are gathered by something which should unite us, commitment to Jesus Christ, most churchmen could not agree on what should be communicated about their Lord. How can there be effective communication when there is such a muddling of message and audience? I know that we are not selling pimple lotion. We are also not a body which simply gathers around a message which is the consensus. However, it is no wonder that small, highly motivated cults and sects can win people. When your major theological thrust is the Holy Spirit, healing, or racial reconciliation, it is easy to know your people's orientation and what your message is. Without this kind of high profile approach, many of us are understandably caught in confusion. However, the people of God are merely a microcosm of the fragmentation that is now infesting our society. Our problem is not unique.

Mass media ministry, then, is a way by which the local community of faith can better understand itself. You will be amazed at how much insight into your church the cadre of people working in radio and television will have. "Rap Around" as a model suggests that perhaps the answers to the problems facing the society may be discovered in the problems themselves as persons encounter a life of faith. This kind of recycling of problems back into themselves has emerged again and again in my work with mass media. We have often looked outside our experiences for an answer. Theologically, Christians share the belief that God is with us now, as he is God with us before and after. Time is tricky. We often get hung up on the linear concepts of where we are located in space. It is within this concept that we must work to deal with the present. The probes of those who lived before (history) and the dreams for the future (hope) are interlocked in this celebration of joy and sorrow now. "Rap Around" has continually been renewed from within the web of its message and its people, within the medium of radio.

I don't want to mislead you. There are lots more wrinkles in this story of the past two years. It is so easy to share another person's experience and then later become discouraged because his example seems so good. I guess that this is the natural process of communicating with our past. Our filters of hope screen out that which was painful or fragmenting.

"Rap Around" has had its share of routine calls. Some of the calls were just boring. Others were put-ons by funny people. Many people in the audience did not understand what I was trying to do, and yet, out of the nearly five thousand letters I have received only two have been critical. One letter felt that the problems were not serious enough for our consideration. The other was from a parent who felt that the problems were too deep for his twelve-year-old son who listened faithfully each week.

There have been times when I have had to rap with my brothers and sisters in the faith about the kind of ministry I have been doing. I am doing this show for a commercial station. It is not entered in the log as a religious show. The fifty to seventy thousand listeners come back each week because the show moves to a secular rhythm they like. I must continually struggle with the tension between the message couched in traditional religious language and the enacted Word of God which is known in the now, through various media. I don't think that we ever will resolve this tension. If the gap doesn't seem to be present in your everyday life, you are either fully into sainthood or you are fooling yourself. In most cases, it is the latter.

F. YOUNG ADULTS

This is the part of demographics most coveted by broadcasters. These are the folk somewhere in the age range from eighteen to forty. They get different kinds of labels. Some radio people call them contemporary listeners. These are the folk who are spending money. It may not always be theirs, yet through credit or extension terms they are buying cars, houses, and lots of bits and pieces—items that make up the American economy. Who knows what such a cross section of people desires? These folk are a multilayered group. Some of them feel like music only at certain times, without much rap. At other times they like to cut back into the top-forty sound to find the new stuff that is just hitting.

The church has been pushed to meet these needs. There was a time when many churchmen would just laugh and say about the young couples who didn't show up in church after years of church school: "They will be back when they have children." I don't know. I am afraid that those who come back in that context are there for the wrong reasons. The young adult age span is critical. The husband and wife family patterns are battled out in this time slot. The church usually plays no role at all in these times of mini-crisis. The church usually says to the young person fresh from college and newly into a career: "You are welcome to join our existing structure." In some sense our churches should be affirming to these folk that their role as part of the body of Christ can bring something fresh to our church life. "How can we change our structure or style as a church to proclaim the Good News in such a way as to bring you into our midst?"

As I have suggested earlier, the radio station does seek to know what the audience can add to its life. It is eager to change its structure to please its audience. It is seeking this interconnection between message and audience for a very different reason than would the church.

Well, the world (including the mass media) is massaging and caring for the young adult's material needs. However, single young adults are in a particularly difficult position. They are often socially isolated in big cities or small towns. The couple-circles are just not open to them. A number of so-called underground FM stations have been programming to this sector. At first these urban stations were noted for raunchy, free-form formats. A host with a very natural voice would spin LP cuts which were not heard among the top forty or on an easy listening station. There was an anti-establishment, independent style to the jocks. These formats have given way to a tightly controlled version of the top-forty station. The big difference between the young adult station and the above ground rock station is that in most situations there is now less talk. Many of these stations even have a rotation mix similar to the rock stations (new release, LP cut, golden oldie, etc.). The young adult or contemporary listener seems to like the three-record sweep and twenty-word transition to next music sweep. Most top-forty rockers have a lot of chatter.

FM is a music environment which is modern, and yet not intrusive like the AM personality jock can be. It is easy to use the FM station as a medium for talk and for a lot of other social contexts. The more mature audience has a lot of concerns which can be met through this medium.

As mentioned earlier, there are some folk who switch back and forth between the FM station and the rocker. Perhaps there are not as many portable FMs around as AMs. Maybe one also likes to peek back at the past as he moves toward maturity. There is also a timelessness to FM that is not obvious on the AM side. Maybe these two faces of radio are really very different media. Stereo FM certainly contains a number of features which are different from the typical AM station.

1. "For What It's Worth"

Tom Bender, a creative religious broadcaster in Detroit, has been experimenting with this medium for young adults. At first his show, "For What It's Worth," focused on raps and music about religion. Perhaps a guest would come by, and they would rap with telephone callers about aspects of theology and ethics. The show touched on some personal aspects of lifestyle, and the whole thing really exploded with excitement. The callers seemed eager to share themselves with a caring and intelligent person. It would seem that many young adults are interested in themselves. This can, of course, be a very self-centered life-style. However, people must be met where they are. Tom is pursuing this probe of his audience' concern.

2. "Word and Music"

Another interesting concept for local radio usage is "Word and Music." This service is developed by TRAFCO (the United Methodist mass media folk) as a scripting service. The weekly units provide reflective copy about the contemporary and ancient music. A local pastor reads the material and plays the musical selections. In many cases, the host may change some of the copy to fit his needs and approach. The group sponsoring this show subscribes to the service. It has been quite popular among adult listeners.

3. "The Hive"

Some of the formats suggested under the youth-programming section have application in this discussion. The sound collage approach has been very popular in a number of programming situations. "The Hive" is a good example of this kind of format. Jack Ridl and Paul Piendl hosted the hour long sound experience. Each show was built around a theme. LP cuts, poetry, recorded comedy, voice actualities were carefully intermixed around the topic. An interesting feature of the show was the original theological humor done by Paul and Jack. The show was broadcast at 1:00 in the morning over a rock station which wanted to pick up the late night adult. An important production note is that the show was mixed and edited by a sixteen-year-old high school student, Bob Mayo. Sometimes Jack and Paul just came up with a theme. They would come in and do the comedy and poetry tracks. The student would then select the music and produce the whole show. Often a creative seminary student, Marcia Miscall, would do the final editing and timing.

The pace and scope of the show surprised and delighted the audience. Themes such as junk, America, and home were explored. Bob would sometimes mix different versions of the same song to give the show unexpected color. "The Hive" tried to combine personal needs with variety and interest in sound which would appeal to the audience. Similar tightly produced shows can be found in many market areas. You simply need the creativity of a few good people. Most stations will release production time once you have established the kind of rapport and trust which we discussed earlier. However, you may have a more difficult time finding the kind of theologically sensitive persons who are attuned to the pop material (music, poetry, comedy, etc.) than getting a station to cooperate.

This is a good point from which to reintroduce the recycling or feedback process discussed in connection with "Rap Around." If it is a problem to reach young adults, why not use them to solve the difficulty? Perhaps they could create the format for ministering to their peers through radio. This way of extending the faith through a preevangelistic use of radio is suggestive as to how the local church might work with young adults. The process of doing media is an actualization of our lives in faith. We have often worked to get something *done* without recognizing that the *process* is the essence of the Christian life. The kind of community needed for mass media programming is an excellent occasion for a manifestation of the Christian community. This kind of intermix breaks down the fragmentation we encourage in most of our church programming. We tend to separate the activities of the faith into isolated segments: worship on Sunday at 11:00, study on Sunday at 10:00, fellowship on occasional Wednesday evenings, mission work project on occasion, and other random activity. After Pentecost the young church gathered in groups which celebrated all aspects of their life together (Acts 2:39-42). When the ministry to young adults or others is pursued through mass media, this reconciliation between the parts of a life through faith should be recognized.

4. "The Personal Line"

Another phone-call format is also suggested by the young adult's situation. Many of the typical talk shows could be restructured in existing time slots to have the kind of thrust that we are talking about. For instance, one all-talk station was convinced through a series of complex approaches to open up two hours of regular broadcast time for "The Personal Line." Baptist minister, John Paul Pro, has an extraordinary talent for combining counseling skills with his Christian concern. We obtained a guest appearance for him on the station. We then took the tape and edited it down to the kind of format we desired. After much encouragement from the station, John became a regular guest on Monday evenings. The regular host handled the phones.

This kind of strategy could be used to get programming for young mothers. Imagine a sensitive child psychologist being a regular guest in such a format. Such an area as marital counseling might be covered in such a design. The station would get a good audience response, and the church could provide trained and theologically sensitive persons as guests.

Much creative work needs to be done in this rich area. The young adults have great needs and every resource should be brought to bear on the use of radio to reach them. A healthy young adult ministry in the local church can develop viable radio formats for this ministry.

G. MINORITY PROGRAMMING

This sector of programming could really apply to every person in medialand. However, there are certain groups which seem to be passed over when radio programming is designed. I remember being in a program manager's office one day. We were brainstorming possible format ideas. I suggested that an area of real concern was the aged and was about to launch into an extensive explanation of the idea I had when he cut me short. "We do not program to old people. They can listen if they want. However, you are not going to reach out to win that audience." Ironically, much of this station's audience was made up of the older citizens. He was reacting to a significant factor in media programming. The older person doesn't spend much money and so advertising is hard to come by for stations and shows that cater to them. A good example of this market factor can be seen in the demise of the Red Skelton and Jackie Gleason shows. These programs had good ratings. However, the demographic breakdown showed a strong audience of older people. While it seems inexcusable in terms of utilizing human resources, the old are often castoffs in our society. In fact, even the church does not really feed the mature member the way he deserves to be nurtured. A few congregations are expanding their ministry to this valuable sector of the church, but only a few so far.

The very young spend their time with TV. There is little on radio for them. Though blacks and other ethnic groups have not had consistent access to radio, there are some ethnic stations in large urban areas. Many stations try to have token miniority representation on the station staff. Yet, if someone claims that they are not being fairly represented, the station will usually let him say his piece in a talk show. However, there should be a style of doing media which enables the minorities or forgotten folk to create their own expressions of humanity.

My experience with community-produced radio programming suggests that just about anyone with the right kind of creative support can extend his humanity through media. We have touched upon teen-produced shows in our earlier discussion. From my experience, I think that groups of angry people could be enabled to create a powerful sound extension of their concern. The process of providing this hard-hitting message would help them restructure their own thinking about the problem. It is funny how the process of producing mass media programming gives you new ways of looking at yourself and those around you. Such community-centered production may only become a reality if the church can nurture these kinds of mass media folk.

Supplementary producers are appreciated by local stations when it is realized that they will take responsibility for getting the show finished. This style of releasing potentiality in others should be part of the evangel who sees himself as a messenger of the Good News. It is very hard to midwife the rebirth of another. We are tempted to force the new creation to take life according to our structures. It just can't be this way. The occasion of mass media again reminds the people of God that it is their job to enable a process to which God gives the direction. In just about every aspect of our daily lives people are trying to force us to do things according to their predetermined agenda. We must talk, act, and respond according to the goals prescribed by them. Faith and media should not be this way. In the hands of a person secure in Christ, such media and faith are free.

H. SPECIALS

The church year suggests all kinds of special programming. Even the most secular station will want something special for Christmas or Passover. Many stations aired the musical *Jesus Christ Superstar* during the past couple of years. Some stations ran it on both Christmas and Easter. One station (KQV) added voice tracks at key points to give the program more bite and reality.

Good Friday has been troublesome to stations. The smaller stations may pick up the local ecumenical services which usually run from noon to 3:00 P.M. This is usually bad radio. A station in Erie had a moving three-hour program. It all came about because of Tom McLaren. He was a local pastor who represented the

local ministerial association to the stations. He suggested that they take the three hours and use spiritually
sensitive music from the top two hundred records. He
found that a number of popular records actually had
religious messages. Tom also noted that it was the
"sound glue" between records which gave the programming a particular character. He produced a series
of spot materials to hold the three hours together. He
used the one-minute prayers of Malcolm Boyd with
Charlie Bird playing in the background. He got permission to read selections from Carl Burke's book, *God
Is for Real, Man* (New York: Association Press, 1966).
This retelling of biblical stories in street language is
quite moving.

Tom also produced five fantastic spots. They were
an intermix of voice tracks, a section of song, sound
effects, and his voice-over. He used the then-popular
song "Abraham, Martin, and John," as the thrust which
recaptured the assassinations of Lincoln, King, and
Kennedy. "It is funny how Good Friday keeps happening all the time," made the tie-in with the season. This
moving series of spots just about blew the engineer's
mind. "I am not religious . . . I don't go to church very
much. But I can see what you are doing, and this is
the most exciting thing I have ever heard!" Tom is a
creative fellow. His relationship with the station was
very good. There was mutual respect. The response to
this show was stunning. He was asked if he would do
the news for them on the weekends.

The special-season programming possibilities are
great. Stations are receptive to creative ways in which
such shows can be done. It is for the Christian to
develop the concepts for this fleshing-out of his
faith. We can not fall back into criticism of mass media
unless we are willing to help develop better pro-

gramming. Our message is so rich with possibilities. When the Good News encounters the human situation, the intermix brings such exciting results. We must get into the message of the whole Christian year and let it explode as it confronts the now. The means available for bringing together these two factors have never been as extensive as they are now.

Another dimension to the "special" approach to radio programming centers around human issues. For instance, several years ago the drug problem was just starting to overtake our community. The rock station was very concerned about it. I gathered a creative group of churchmen together with the program director. We developed a concept by which we would produce a five-hour drug special along with a heavy play of public service drug spots. Many of us went out into the community and did interviewing. The show unfolded with power. Our audience opening night was enormous. We combined twenty-minute, taped segments of rap and music with live phone calls. The show received wide attention, and even the President sent a message. It was the beginning of some community work on this vast problem. The show later won many national awards, but it could never have had the power and outreach it achieved without the churchmen. This kind of interrelationship between the church and the station has much promise in every market area. "The Drugged Generation" is just one example of the kind of thing which can be done in this partnership.

It is possible that you can even help the stations understand what the problems in your community are. Where a station is failing to meet the needs of its community it is usually the result of its inability to discover those needs. Stations want to serve their people, and many appreciate the church's aid in getting at the listener in aconstructive way.

I. CHURCH STATIONS

One large suburban church suddenly became concerned with the church's role in radio. The first thing they did was set up a high level committee of laymen. These folks conducted an exhaustive study of the possibilities of getting their own station. The men and women on this task force traveled all over the country in the quest for their data. They even visited with one of the FCC commissioners in Washington. Their overview was impressive. They saw the need for a community station which would facilitate some low-profile theological goals. The kind of communication which that community needed wasn't being provided in any other way. They faced a number of problems. It would cost a lot. How could they come up with fresh locally produced programming instead of just using taped material produced somewhere else? These folks are still struggling with this proposal.

A church that has moved through this process quite successfully is the Market Square Presbyterian Church in Harrisburg, Pennsylvania. In 1962 WMSP-FM came on the air as a classical music station. This kind of music programming was greatly needed in the area. The music became the context within which the religious message was shared in small bits and pieces. A particular audience could be nurtured spiritually in this way.

The Market Square Presbyterian Church serves an older community in the downtown area of the Pennsylvania state capitol. It was searching for a ministry that could bring the Good News to its urban complex. The station will soon be boosted to fifty thousand watts. A communication committee of the church assumes the responsibility for the development and pursuit of the business dimension of the station. The church currently provides about thirty thousand dollars a year for the operation of the station. Other funds come from the public.

The station has a full-time, professional manager, which is one of the key factors about WMSP. Roy Humphrey is a radio professional who has combined his experience in the media with a term of service in the mission field. He actively involves members of the community and the church in the programming thrust. The station is now seriously considering an all-night program to minister to those who are having problems. The tentative design would utilize a regular host and rotating guest clergy. People are invited to call in with problems. If something comes up which might demand personal counseling, the caller will be invited to come to the station for help at that time.

One of the exciting proposals before this station is the possible use of the FM subchannel for special programming to the blind. People in the community who cannot read would be equipped with special receivers. The subchannel would beam a separate program format to them. Popular magazines would be read, special tips for their life-style would be shared, and a community calling program could be developed in relationship to the radio input.

WMSP has not become narrow and parochial in its outreach. Some "Christian" stations are tempted to become as myopic as some commercial outlets. It seems inescapable that Christian theology on mass media must be freed to touch the lives of mass listeners and viewers. Proclamation must be found in the incarnation of the Good News.

Your church may be in the position to follow this path of obtaining a radio license. However, it seems that the greatest opportunity for outreach is still with the commercial stations. With the proper sensitivity (in terms of theology and mass media) the possibilities for doing radio in your community are vast.

V. OTHER ALMOST-MASS-MEDIA SOUND SYSTEMS

A. COLLEGE STATIONS

There are a number of radio outlets open in the church community. Many colleges have stations which are broadcast for only a few blocks. Yet, if the system for communication exists, it can be used to reach people. Often such stations are poorly operated. The students really need an enabling ministry around this outlet. You have to move carefully in this academic maze, for there is often a lot of politics involved in anything that the college students create for public distribution. However, churchmen are accustomed to working in these contexts. These audio environments are excellent for experimentation. The station may be so bad that anything will improve it. It might be good training ground for the churchmen also. By offering to fill a regular time slot you may be able to minister to the college community while you learn.

B. INTERCOM SYSTEMS

There are other intercom types of broadcasting for large work or study complexes. A number of high schools are letting students do programming over the intercom during lunch periods. This is a good place to work. Much of your work may not be apparent on the surface. You are not undertaking this ministry to get publicity. You are enabling others to struggle with a communication which has depth and power. The fact that you participate in the students' attempt to broadcast music in their high school will say a great deal about the church's love for young people. Your aid in their development may provide the basis of a relationship out of which may come more overt theological communication. It is the substructure of human exchange from which comes the kind of communication which enables others to experience the love of Jesus Christ.

One high school in Ohio has a very difficult transportation situation. Because of financial problems the district consolidated into one high school. Some students have to travel three hours a day on buses. An enterprising school official was able to get a government grant to explore the means of using radio input for the students during the bus ride. Now he is searching for something to program.This is where the creative churchman should be able to step in and help. What a fantastic opportunity to touch the lives of the students. The use of mass media keeps coming down to the creative intermix of message and listener.

C. FM SIDE BAND

Another derivative communication system is the FM side band or subchannel. Certain stations have the right to sublease bands for FM usage. These airwave spaces are often rented out by the licensee for special group communication systems. For instance, such broadcast bands can carry a continuous music service. The receiver must be specially tuned to pick up the signal. The cost of side band rental is not unreasonable. One regional ecumenical broadcast group experimented with using this limited radio communication system for continued theological education. The plan was to have churches subscribe to the service by the year. Four hours of programming would be broadcast each day. Lectures, study courses, famous preachers, news, and the like could be piped down the electric network. For eighty dollars a year the pastor in the rural area could receive daily input from the latest in theological publications, events, and developments.

For a number of reasons this experiment came to an end without any conclusive evaluation. The promotion and programming developments were inconsistent. Many pastors greatly appreciated the service. Others found it restrictive to be at the receiver at the same time each day. This nurturing use of a mass media system could be invaluable for any kind of evangelism. If those who are called to reach others are not fed, there will be no harvest. In fact, the biggest danger in encouraging any kind of campaign to reach out to others is that we won't be able to deliver when they do come. If the massmediaman is touched by the message of Christ, how does he grow in the faith once inside the church? It is a bit discouraging to compare the relationship between the number of visitors a church may have and the number who come to stay permanently. Continuing education for clergy and laymen is the key to the depth and growth of the church. Mass media systems for teachers and preachers is the wave of the future.

D. THE AUDIO CASSETTE

One convenient extension of mass media is the audio cassette. This compact, self-contained tape is enclosed in a plastic case the size of a cigarette package. It will hold up to two hours of recorded material. The machine that plays it is inexpensive (from twenty-five dollars up). The cassette recorder will play on batteries or an electric outlet. The machines are light and small. This means that a person can carry one with him and listen through an earplug on buses, airplanes, anywhere. A number of companies are following the lead of Thesis Theological Cassettes (P.O. Box 11724, Pittsburgh, Pennsylvania, 15228) and are providing theological software for continuing education. Thesis, for instance, provides lectures and discussions by the world's leading theologians and churchmen. This means that a pastor or layman can deepen his understanding of the faith at the time that is most convenient for him. This audio cassette offers the local church many possibilities for its outreach and ministry. With the simple editing techniques discussed on pages 37-45, a local church can create an edited version of a worship service for shut-ins on reel-to-reel tape and then dub copies onto cassettes for the individual to use at home. The playback machine with no recording facilities is even cheaper than the recorder.

One pastor makes effective use of the cassette and

reaches out to his people by recording a personal message to a person about to undergo surgery. He has found that the night before an operation is often quite lonely for the patient after everyone has left. When he is about to leave, he presents this tape and asks the patient to play it later if he should be lonely. Upon recovery from surgery, one elderly lady bought the church a dozen cassette machines. She felt that everyone who is sick should have the benefit of this extension of the ministry. This example well illustrates how a new medium in the hands of a creative brother simply expands an ancient ministry of the church.

E. MA BELL'S CHILD: THE PHONE

Another sound medium is quite important to our discussion—the phone. This medium is often misused by people, and a lot of pastors don't realize that this universal form of communication can broaden their outreach. If most pastors would only spend an hour a day in the creative use of the phone, their ministries would be expanded vastly. A minister can be warm, yet disciplined, in talking to folk. For instance, when a person is passing thrugh the post-grief period after having lost a loved one, care is important. Often sympathetic friends shower him with care at the time of the funeral, but then disappear. A daily phone call and one visit a week from the pastor would be better than a daily visit. He might call and say that he is on the way to the hospital (or whatever he is doing next), but just happened to think of the person. The pastor has set the limits of the call, and he is also showing his real care by reaching out to the person.

The phone can also be used creatively in the hands

of laymen. In one church I served, a woman was highly trained in writing and in office work before she went blind. She was very sensitive to the needs of others, and became a key information point in our outreach program. She would regularly call those who needed special care. Her input report to the pastor would reveal how much additional work he had to do with particular persons at a given point. It was amazing how she could summon a congregation on a few days' notice. The church attendance/membership ratio was fantastic in this small congregation. It was in large measure due to her work with the people via the phone. Her warmth and care were amplified through the phone.

Radio and its related sisters are special media. I guess that you can tell that I love radio. It can do so much with so little. It is totally accessible to the creative Christian. Radio and its kin are open to the kind of help and support we can give. This audio medium is waiting to be of service to those sharing Christ's love. It just needs Christians to utilize it.

VI. DOING TELEVISION AND ITS RELATED SYSTEMS

A. THE MEDIUM

It came. We saw it. It conquered. At least, so it seems. More than 50 percent of urban media market people now own color TVs. We have all been swept into this major communication web. Some folk still grumble about the limits television has placed on our imaginations. However, the big eye has also unleashed new vistas. We are a global village in which the broadest range of cultural experience is now ours. We are different from what we were. Our children are different from what we were. Their children will be different from what they are now. Our nerve endings have become public, and we are now interrelated as a new media family. The demands and pressures of this new awareness are sometimes almost unbearable. We get

overloaded. We just can't conduct all this human energy. We mentally select or sort out input to fit the structural patterns we embrace. This subjective reality
differs from one person to another. This divides us
from our brothers and sisters. The more our exposure
to the world increases, the more our selection de-
creases.

This powerful creature is still a baby in the hands
of its parents. In any case, television is merely radio
with pictures. Most local shows (with few exceptions)
are "couch shows." Even the news production is limited, having some film and a rigid set. It is often em-
barrassing to discover how few original productions
local stations create each week. A lot of commercials
may be cooked up in the studios. However, television
chiefly lives off the things that come down the pike
from other production centers and from the networks.

Many things have been said very well by others
about the problems of television in our age. Parents
groups are organizing to pressure for a more responsible use of the medium for their children. From time to
time people get uptight about violence on the tube.
These things are quite important. It is good that people
are looking critically into the dimensions of television
programming. However, there are revolutionary things
happening through television which are more pressing
than the messages they think they are communicating.

If just one small aspect of life, like the perception
of time, is changed, it is amazing what happens to
us. For instance, institutions of our society have chosen
to transmit their history and content to us in huge
blocks of input. Lectures, sermons, and other forms
of communication tend to be an hour or more in
length. However, the electric mass media have upset
this. Just log a typical television hour, and you will

be surprised to note that there may be as many as fifteen bits of communication thrust at you. No solid block of input is over twelve or fifteen minutes in length. Most of the messages are extremely short and varied. Just focus on the commercial clutter at the commercial break. You may find several ads, a station identification, and two public service announcements. These inputs will have come to you in a wide variety of pace and with different visual styles. There may have been a humorous soap ad, a shocking spot on rat control, a naturalistic outdoor ad for a hair product, and a tender mother-and-child commercial for baby lotion. The viewer is flooded not only with sound, as in radio, but also with visual images. We must sort out and make sense of these stimuli.

It is interesting to take a group of people through a visual and sound experience which moves them from slow-paced input to rapid stimulation. Folk can learn to pick up more in a shorter space of time with this kind of media conditioning in the same way as persons who have had a rapid reading course, where words and clusters of words are flashed on a screen at an ever faster rate of speed. The advertiser has used this principal when he spaces thirty and ten second versions of his original one-minute spot. After a number of viewings, the audience is able to get the same impression from the thirty-second ad as they did from the original sixty-second one. Still, later the ten-second spot can get the same message across. This is not to say that increased speed of comprehension or stimulation is good or bad. It is just the way things are.

Problems arise for all of us when we move from this sensual mountaintop of audio-visual media into the valley of listening to long blocks of information or historical recital. What happens to the kids who leave the speed of "Sesame Street" for the subsensual environment of most classrooms? Television teases us with involvement and community. However, it leaves us to cope with institutional experiences which are downers or lows in terms of stimulation. Many people think that a life of low stimulation is better for man. However, the time for such a choice is past. To cut one's self off from the electric generator of mass media is to deny the whole of modern society. This may not be a bad decision. However, most of us just can't survive in the world without plugging into this environment for news, entertainment, and comfort. This is cheap community. And yet, for many this is all the companionship they have.

Some probes have been conducted concerning modern man's relationship to television. A control group was studied in terms of the need for TV. The startling results suggest that many people are addicted to the tube. Their whole lives fall apart when they deny themselves television watching. Marriages were threatened and lives took a swing for the worse. There seem to be similarities here between drug usage and electric media. Some interesting therapy is now being done with drug users by having them create media.

Programming on television raises a lot of questions. How much does the content of the program reflect the message that the viewers are actually receiving? Much verbiage has gone down about news stories being handled improperly. Don't be misled by this aspect of media. I think that the total power and influence of television far exceed the individual content items. The intermix of the sound-visual input into a person's home and life as an experience is far more influential than the content of any particular show.

It is hard for the Christian to approach television in a mass media ministry. We can not hitchhike on the insights of the medium the way we can in radio. Television is still a child. It has not been able to explore, discover, or actualize its nature. There are many reasons for this retardation. A good part of the problem is economics. Television is expensive. Sound can be captured anywhere on simple equipment. Visual forms have to be filmed or taped outside of the studio and/ or within it. This is a costly process.

We have suggested that television and radio have changed our chronology. At the same time, the speed demands of this age turn back on the medium and haunt television. TV is one of the most harried of electric media. Newsmen are always running down the halls with bits and pieces of visuals for the show that is on the air. The producers just can't keep up with the appetite of this one-eyed monster. It eats up everything in sight.

Television stations are generally considered either "commercial" or "public." Commercial video channels are supported by advertising revenue. Public outlets are maintained by donations and grants. It is strange that both styles of telecasting seem very similar when viewed from the perspective of distance. Public television usually has simpler equipment and a few liberated programs. However, when you look at the local stations' drives for audience and financial stability, both breeds of cat are in the same corner. The ratio of creative local programming to canned shows from the outside is quite close for both kinds of television.

The same dynamics tend to work in the local churchman's relationship to the stations. There may be a different audience profile between public and commercial stations in some markets. The public station can give you some clues on this matter if you pursue it. I have worked with stations having both kinds of financial support. In some cases, opportunities for creativity are more plentiful on the public video medium. However, the lack of funds tends to minimize this factor in some markets having public stations. Good folks run these brands of television.

The local station produces programming within a narrow scope of possibilities. Most of its shows come from somewhere else. What is done locally is probably video-taped in the studio. The facilities in many markets are quite restricted. Stations are limited to one or two cameras instead of three. The special effects on most studio control boards are rarely used. This is one of the reasons so many religious programs tend to be couch shows. If you ask for something out of the ordinary you will probably get a claim that it is impossible. This flat answer need not discourage you too much. It is the creative Christian's task to work through the limitations in a given local situation.

In every radio and television market area there will be religious broadcasters who buy time. These folk must serve an audience. They are usually able to pay for their time out of contributions sent in from the area. However there is a serious question in my mind about who is being reached. Perhaps these time purchasers are able to do something valid for church people who are not being fed well enough by their faith community. However, I am still concerned for the uncommitted person who has not been accustomed to the style and language patterns of the traditional faith community. Will anybody reach out to him?

B. THE GUEST GAMBIT

Most stations have one or more talk shows, of which one may have a religious format. This is a good place for another important strategy factor. If you have several radio and television stations in your area, you will find that there are several shows which regularly use guests. One of the most difficult tasks facing a producer is the booking or placement of fresh people for every show. Any producer will simply run out of guests. This is one reason why you see so many of the same guests on local talk shows. The producer finds an articulate person and keeps going back to this guest again and again.

Marshall McLuhan has suggested that information will be the key to power in the future. Those who can retrieve needed information and interface it with current problems and needs will have enormous power. On a mini-scale the same is true now in most local situations. In Pittsburgh, I have developed a file on about one thousand people. These are folk who have something to say and are not overexposed by media appearances. I let my friends at the stations know that I could get guests for them at any time. At first, I was called only in emergencies. The scheduled person had not shown up, and taping would begin in an hour. The twenty-five talk shows in our area were soon getting regular aid from my office. There was never any credit given for this help. However, we soon found that we were putting more and more people on these shows. In some cases, producers would call and say that they had just been assigned the task of doing a special on a certain topic. We would then brainstorm the show. I would furnish him with many names of people who might have something important to say about the subject. The special would be aired, and a large proportion of the guests featured would be people from my file. This is a subtle way of influencing television programming, so don't underestimate the power of this strategy.

A few words should be said about seeking and placing guests on these shows. You have to realize that the medium of television is very unstable. The equipment is always breaking down. There are many points at which the technology can fail. This means that you will be asked to come early for your appearance and will often end up waiting for a long time.

I will never forget the justice of state supreme court who was to be a guest on the teen television show we produced. He came at the time we suggested and found that we were not ready to go. He stormed out in a fit of rage. He returned in twenty minutes to find that there had been an equipment breakdown. Again he left in disgust. This went on three or four times. We finally were ready to start and did the show with him. If you want to work in the realm of television you must be prepared for the technological time gap. I have experienced this same problem in New York at the taping of a network show. Those responsible for the content of the show have no control over the technical part of it. Don't blow your cool when you are caught waiting. This is just the nature of the medium.

A couple of years ago I was a guest on a teen show taped in Jacksonville, Florida. It was a couch-type show with a host and five teens. I had brought a slide and sound insert to be used as the beginning of our discussion. We finished the show and everyone had left, when the engineer came in to say that something had gone wrong. The show just taped could not be aired.

We had wasted the evening. My schedule did not permit me to come back the next day. In these situations the guest must be gracious and understanding. The media person knows that such a response indicates a professional understanding of television.

When you select guests, try to find persons who have earned the right to speak. Television needs people who have something to say and who say it well. This does not mean that the person has to be a great public speaker. It does mean that you choose persons who are speaking out of their experience.

You must also match guest with the show. As we have mentioned earlier there are different ways a host may handle guests. Some hosts simply want controversy. This is fine if your guest can handle this. I remember visiting one talk show where the host flipped through the pages of my book and without having read it asked me, "How can you justify writing a religious book filled with sex and drugs?" His statement, of course, had nothing to do with the book in his hands. He was just trying to exploit the situation. I usually try to give the host simple materials to help him in his job. A clear and simple résumé should be prepared in terms of the focus of the interview. This means that you lift out of the guest's background the things which will lead into the discussion at hand. You might even prepare some general areas of discussion and give these to the guest. These should not be canned questions. You had better pick the area of the discussion's thrust, or you might be amazed at what a host will do with the guest you supplied.

It is most important that your guest contribute toward making the show good. Most producers want good shows and good guests. This does not mean that a guest has to say what the host wants, or even be controversial. However, most stations like lively shows. You will distract them from the message you are trying to establish if the guest is boring or not interested in the whole process. Once you have established your- self as a source of good media guests, there will be little difficulty getting just about anyone you want on television in your area. It is amazing how seldom churches use mass media in this way.

C. SPOTS ON THE TUBE

Your easiest introduction to a station is in connec- tion with spots. As mentioned earlier, most of the larger denominations are now producing radio and television spots. The TV material has been particularly good. Almost every dimension of faith and life has been explored. The spots are often very gripping, and stations generally like the good ones. They are either getting these in the mail now, or your local radio and television man for the council of churches is taking them to the station. If you don't have such a full-time worker, you better have the radio and television com- mittee of your church take up this facet of media min- istry. The Broadcast and Film Commission (see p. 48) can assist you in this. After your committee has pre- viewed a particular series of spots, go to the station and get reactions. If the program manager agrees to run them, provide backup support through the church bulletins and the like. You might even use the spots in your study program to provide a tie between mass media and the local religious education task.

Some stations offer community public service spot opportunities. They may make up a special slide with the local cause and the call letters of the station together. At the station break they read the ten-second sound spot and show the slide. You will be surprised to see how these short bits and pieces of input will stick in people's minds.

There can be a lot of heartache doing this kind of ministry. One summer ten pastors in our area spent many days working on an experimental set of spots for a local television station. We wrote and produced five one-minute spots each. These were going to be used during the broadcast day. The station even gave one pastor 35mm film so that he could shoot slides in the community. Special sound tracks were produced for some of the spots. One minister, Father Donald Hays, developed his spots around the use of the chessboard. Another minister had the phone as the main focus of the messages. Well, we produced them, and they were never aired. The management was afraid this style would take too much production time. But don't be discouraged. There is a lot of satisfaction in this kind of ministry, along with the problems.

D. "THE PLACE"

My first experience with local television production started out with a fairly ambitious project. "The Place" was a joint venture of WQED-TV and the Council of Churches of the Pittsburgh area. A group of high school students were pulled together and a production team developed. In the course of the show's four years of production, several talented director-producers worked with us. Our structure differed from year to year. Generally students took the responsibility for different areas of the production. One cadre would audition the rock groups and other talent. Another group would develop the discussions with special guests. We also had a drama group at one time in the show's life. Two shows were taped every other week. We would have one day in which to do the two half-hour shows. The show's setting was a coffeehouse, and I was a proprietor. It was my task to provide continuity to what the high school students were doing in that environment. The twenty-five students who developed the show grew with the experience. It was impressive to see the change in them as they learned to work in the medium of television. A typical rundown of a show looked like this:

THE PLACE (Program #18)		Tape: Sat., Feb. 1, 1969, 3:00 p.m. Air: Wed., Feb. 26, 1969, 7:30 p.m. Sat., Mar. 1, 1969 2:00 p.m.		
SEGMENT TIME	29:00 BACK TIME	AUDIO	VIDEO	AREA
2:30	26:30	Music open (piano)	Mark McNary & titles	Right center & shelf unit
:30	26:00	Host open	Benson (in fencing gear)	Foreground
10:00	16:00	Fencing demonstration	Benson & West Virginia University Fencing Club	Foreground
3:00	13:00	Music feature (guitar)	Morgan Donato (original number)	Left balcony
5:30	7:30	Discussion "Drugs"	Benson, Mrs. Mulvihill, & 2 guests	Right balcony
5:00	2:30	Music feature (piano)	Mark McNary (original number)	Right center
:20	2:10	Host close	Benson (camera 3)	Right balcony
2:10	—0—	Music close (guitar)	Morgan Donato & credits	Left balcony & shelf unit

We even developed fairly complex technical projects. On Halloween we would use special television magic to change me instantly from a mild mannered host into a monster. We would sometime feature guests like Eugene McCarthy and Father Ian Mitchell. We even had a then-unknown folk singer named Don McLean ("American Pie"). Occasionally the station gave us the freedom to do remote shows from locations around town. The visit to a local church-sponsored coffeehouse was the first show I hosted. The county fair was another location show we did. The superintendent of the public schools, judges, a black policeman, and a number of other interesting and important figures were featured in the context of young people. The value and excitement of good conversation could be experienced by those at home.

"The Place" was an interesting concept. It soon provided the motivation for numerous coffeehouse ministries in the Pittsburgh area. As Director of Youth Ministry for the Council of Churches, I would help the local churches develop this kind of work with youth. A radio version of "The Place" followed this multi-faceted media ministry. The radio show is still on the air.

As a television show, "The Place" was on six other educational stations in Pennsylvania during its last year of existence. At one time it won a national award for the show that best involved the community. This concept suggests that young people are capable of assisting in the production of mass media programming. This is an important factor so often overlooked when a discussion of the television media is undertaken.

"The Place" got trapped in its own history. It did not change the way it should have. There is always the danger that a successful program will continue to repeat itself. We were aired on Wednesdays at 7:30 P.M. and Saturdays at 2:00 P.M. We even beat "Batman" in the ratings at one time during its hey-day. Those of us closest to the show wanted change. However, it was not possible within the boundaries in which we worked. It was best that the show did leave the air. It had accomplished something valuable, and we were grateful.

E. "COLLAGE"

There are other ideas for doing creative youth pro-gramming on television. We can assume that the usual couch format of adults and kids talking is in every-body's mind. Rob McClure and I designed (but so far haven't produced) a show which we called "Collage." We wanted to take a group of young people and have them design a huge wall collage in response to a pop-ular record. The collage wall would then be video-taped under the direction of the young people. There would be a match-up between the collage and the song used as a sound track.

The set would be some warm environment where the young people and the artist who recorded the song could relax. The tape would be played. The artist and the teens would then rap about what they had both created. There would be no host. The teens would be meeting the artists as cocreators and not just as fans. Meanings about life could be explored naturally in this format.

F. ROCK FEAST

Another useful format for a youth program would be the rock festival setting. Imagine a series of programs

117

developed around some rock concerts specially designed for the show. The group could be seen not
only on the stage with the large outdoor audience,
but would also be featured in rap sessions with
members of the audience. Performer and fan could
together dig into the meaning of the songs. This show
could capture the freedom of the rock festival, while
giving it additional depth.

One deceptive thing about youth television shows
is that young people are not the only viewers. There
are many adults who watch these shows. Concerning
"The Place," the adults often confessed that they
wanted to find out what young people were thinking.
This is quite important. Perhaps you could design a
youth show which is really an aid for adults. This
means that your focus might be different from what
you had first imagined. In fact, mobile teens do not
sit and watch television all the time, while adults tend
to watch the tube more steadily. Your media ministry
might be directed to parents and other supportive
adults through the youth idiom.

G. CHILDREN'S PROGRAMMING

Television has paid a lot of attention to the children in its audience. The rip-off cartoon shows are now
being pressed to do something more for their viewers.
The pioneer work of shows like "Misterogers Neighborhood" has set standards which are hard to meet. Fred
Rogers is a Presbyterian minister who was developed
a good example of the kind of media ministry I am
talking about. He translates his theological concern
into nontheological language and relationships in
order to reach the young children across the country.

He provides an experience of care and concern on each show. His music is filled with heavy theological concepts. Yet, the lyrics are simple and honest. A few hours with Fred's songs may be one of the best ways to understand this soft or preevangelism approach to media.

A number of people around the country are experimenting with the use of children's programming for theological input. A show like "Tree House" uses more overt faith approaches. Biblical verses, moralistic stories, and the like are used in a puppet and fantasy setting. This show is much "hotter" than the "cool" Misterogers approach. Again, there are some parts of the general audience that welcome this reinforcement of what the child is getting in church school.

"World of Wonder" is a show which has a lower religious profile than "Tree House." Sister Maureen Rodgers and her folk produce this sensitive children's show for WNEM-TV (Saginaw, Michigan). She uses music, puppets, and an imaginative set for this gentle unfolding of life and love for the young child. This local production holds out real hope for others who might want to fill the holes in current programming.

As we have suggested numerous times, so much can be done without funds and experience. Experience you can gain by doing. The financial support is sometimes taken care of as the station meets its own needs. Most stations would be very happy to have their own locally produced children's show. Sister Maureen Rodgers provides the creative spark by which "World of Wonder" becomes a reality. This is the gift which the Christian has to give. The gift, however, must be nurtured in order to become manifest in local media. It has rested dormant for too long.

A group of my friends gathered to produce a chil-

119

dren's show several years ago. A local station indicated some interest. Jack Ridl and Paul Piendl wrote some new songs. Several others developed learning games. We were going to aim at the seven-to nine-year-old child. The show was entitled, "Me." We had planned to use an oriental singer as hostess. One of the most exciting features of the program was the creation of a special character, Heap. We wanted him to move among the children, and they would have to interact with him. He would be moody, bad, or lonely on various occasions. Heap would not talk, he would just be a presence on the set.

We wanted to use real kids in the show. We figured that perhaps fifteen or twenty young people could be on each show. We wanted the kids to wear pajamas. We figured that this way children were dressed for early Saturday morning viewing. All this planning predated "Sesame Street." However, the station at the very last minute refused to go ahead with the project. That's show biz. However, such a collection of creative people is also available in your community. Over against our failure to get the show on the air there are dozens of local groups which have been successful. You will be surprised to learn how many people write music or have other skills. The church never calls on them to share these gifts in a ministry.

There are some good materials which can be dropped into a children's format. The American Lutheran Church, for instance, has a series of animated biblical stories. There is the popular Davey and Goliath series which comes in fifteen-minute segments. The American Bible Society distributes a five-minute series with Annie Vallotton, who did the line drawings for *Good News for Modern Man.* She stands in front of a transparent plastic window, facing the audience as she draws and tells the Bible stories. There are also good spots created for children by several denominations. These and other materials can be worked into a free-flowing format for the younger television audience. Again, the cohesive element for this kind of programming and creativity with existing resources is provided by the Christian who is concerned about his world. These production qualities are not always available to the typical station. Your contribution may be greatly appreciated. It is also possible that your media ministry will be such that you continually discover people of potentiality. Free them to use their gifts for this kind of work. Many people possessing individual gifts for working with children cannot find outlets for these talents. You can enable them to find a setting for their ministry by seeing to it that such a program gets on the air.

H. SPECIALS

The church has been blessed with a number of occasions upon which specials may be based. Christmas, Good Friday, Easter, and a number of quasi-religious days (Memorial Day, etc.) are naturally times for stations to do something special. The opportunities are great for us, because we are the ones who should know something more about these special days than anyone else. However, we have more often than not been unable to give any media form to the celebration of these days. Just look at the one-dimensional attempts at celebrating Christmas in most churches. We are pushed to find new ways to flesh-out the Incarnation in the lives of our people. Mass media creates a great challenge.

One year Tom Ashwell, then Public Affairs Director of KDKA-TV, and I were talking about what we could do for Easter. He told me that they had some excellent time available on Easter afternoon. A special could be aired right after the Leonard Bernstein Children's Concert at 5:30 P.M.—if it were good. We decided to go after something good. Tom has an excellent background in drama. The symbiotic relationship between the Christian Associates of Southwest Pennsylvania and the station at this point was that, by working through this interfaith agency, the station wouldn't have to pay the actors wages. They could also get an original script and a large cast through us, and from them we could get some television experience. The two writers we chose enjoyed the challenge of writing this original material. "The Trial" was the result of our joint efforts. A cast of fifty actors and actresses presented a you-are-there approach to the trial of Jesus. A local judge who is an expert in ancient Jewish law acted as commentator on the process.

We spent twelve hours taping the thirty-minute show. Tom did it in movie fashion. We shot the scenes one by one. We did and redid each one until it was right. The drama was then edited into the final show. This simple concept produced a very moving show. The station has rerun the drama each year since its first production.

One Christmas a special children's show was produced for airing on Christmas morning. We used a talented churchman, Steve Brezzo, who is an extraordinary puppeteer and actor. The thirty-minute show told the Christmas story in a low-keyed and very moving way.

The church has such rich content in its message. Stations will respond positively when they can experience the fact that this message has found media skins into which it fits. The burden rests upon us to make this relationship happen.

I believe that once the church community has really become related to its history there are a number of other special church days that could be shared in mass media. Pentecost could be an exciting television experience, if we really let it take electric form. Ash Wednesday usually gets some attention on the local news because there is a graphic dimension in the ashes some churchmen get on their foreheads. Wherever an honest graphic form comes out of the context of the situation, you have the basis for media usage.

If your church has deep concern about certain matters which cut across the interests of your local community, mass media should be utilized regularly. Let's say that your mission group has uncovered the desperate plight of migrant workers in the area. Television could be an excellent way to arouse concerns of the community. The graphic side of your ministry can be fleshed-out beautifully on television. Most stations will use 35mm slides, if they are shot horizontally and not vertically. The color contrasts must also be quite good. They will project the slides through their slide chain. If you are in the position to get some 16mm film footage of the subject, the station can use it. Most stations will not be able to run 8mm or super-8 film. If you want your slides to run in a particular sequence, be sure to provide a script for the director. In most cases, the station will use any still photos or art work, but be sure that these are large enough for mounting. Glossy or shiny materials reflect light and cause a light problem. A dull finish on the pictures will make things easier.

Just brainstorm how our history of salvation could take on a contemporary visual shape on your local television station. The biblical material is so graphic. It jumps out at you. The more you dig into the study of the text in its original languages the more creative forms are suggested. God is angry. Push a little farther. God's face is red. God's nose is purple. This brilliance is in the Hebrew imagery. The realm of mass media is just challenging us to proclaim our faith in a way consistent with the form of the new media and the content of the past. God has used every form of human sense-experience to incarnate the Good News to his people. This is the kind of ministry we are called to fulfill by the times and by our faith.

I. COUCH SHOWS

Most religious programs on television fall into this bag. A host talks with guests as they sit at a table or on a couch. There are few graphics and no movement. Often these shows will be shot with one camera only. This is the minimum in creative programming. Yet, you will sometimes find yourself in such a situation. Perhaps you can gently expand this concept by introducing stills and slides. The problem will not be a technical one. It will be a production difficulty. Who is going to collect the material for each show? The station won't; they don't have the time. The church should assign a producer who can do the research and re-sourcing for the shows. Extending the visual aspect of the show will help a great deal. Even the use of some prepackaged material may help. Some spots can be used, perhaps even parts of existing religious shows

from national denominations. Why not use a local artist to sketch while the conversation is going on? He
could be giving his visual impression of what is being
said.

Another way to liven up this kind of show is to utilize a number of shorter segments. Perhaps you can
feature several focal points each about six-minutes in
length. This gives the impression of movement and
variety. It will not drop the viewer off by the wayside.
Some features which need to be covered on television
are: people of faith as they function with authenticity
in the world, the spiritual development and growth of
clergymen, family problems and faith, creative Bible
study, ministry to those in need, faith and the news.

It helps to pick the right person to host these religious talk shows. Temperament and communication
ability are important factors in choosing such a person.
Not every clergyman possesses the qualities necessary
for hosting a television show. Small gestures and random eye movement can become very distracting attri-
butes to a media-sensitive audience. Churchmen have
gotten away with a lot of communication sloppiness.
The electric eye catches us in our habits. Television
newsman can do a good job of reading and speaking
to the audience at the same time. Most churchmen
cannot. Clergymen are not taught this kind of discipline. They usually don't have to be on their toes
in this area of personal communication. This is another
example of the message of the Christian faith being
swallowed by old forms and of being incarnated in
new forms. A good host must draw upon his inner
strength and be able to listen. He must draw out the
other person's humanity in such a way that the audience can participate in the guest's personhood. Even

though such a standard may seem high, don't worry. The media's capacity to develop such people is even behind the church's.

One possibility for the couch television show is a news format. Jim Waller has been working on a format which would bring the audience a Today-kind of Sunday morning show. There is little or no television news on Sunday morning. Stations don't like to pay extra to have crews at the station at a time when the audience is not extensive, and usually news is slow on Sundays. This makes it a good time to release special news if you want it on the air. Jim feels that the church would be doing a real service if it could get such a show on the air. World news could be reported in a regular manner. Special segmented features dealing with faith and life could be used. The news dimension of this concept is the fresh aspect. It would give the show a contemporary nature which is often missing. There is little relation to time in most religious programming. We seem to say that it doesn't matter when you see this message. Every other television format strives to meet the viewer now, where he is living. Even the bland situation comedies now deal with racism, women's liberation, and other timely topics.

The biggest problem with these established formats is their lack of flexibility and the limited variety of material covered. We can come up with fifteen or twenty shows, and then we start to run dry. The church nurtures a support system for the production of mass media that can keep its well of creativity filled to the top. We must really draw upon our greatest God-given resource: people. Our folk are the vehicle through which the Holy Spirit works. In so many of our linear plans we have only called upon our leadership. Those in power should do a great deal. However, the electric age is upsetting the traditional top-down approach of serving people. Our biggest resource is the whole community of believers. This means that the mass media process for local folk should rest upon the shoulders of a broad range of procedures.

In most church situations we tap people to do jobs according to their vocation in the world. This sounds very reasonable. But is it? A man may be a banker all day. However, this may not be the focus of his real joy. He may spend all his leisure time in a darkroom. Photography really turns him on. Yet, he is asked by the church to be a trustee. Christ compels us to dig more deeply into the lives of our people. Where do they really come from? You can't tell from their role in the tracking system of the world any longer. They are so much more complex and beautiful than you can imagine. It may be that the church can lift them to new heights of potentiality. Perhaps new skills can be developed and nurtured.

It may sound too mechanical. However, it is unfortunate that we don't dig into the beings of our people and find their sources of life. These rich gifts could then be sorted out in a computer, and we could interface the community's needs with these strengths. This does not mean that we have fulfilled our work when we ask new members to fill out what they would like to do in existing programs. It is so much more than this. We have roads before us that have not yet been traveled. We have tasks before us that have not yet been undertaken. We have new ministries before us that we have not yet discovered. They are there. We have yet to see them. Success will come to those who have ears to hear and eyes to see.

J. DEVOTIONS

In just about every market area clergymen are asked to tape closing devotions for the station. This aspect of religious broadcasting is usually the poorest. Late night talk show hosts have long kidded about the sermonette of the day—with good reason. You have seen them: The poor clergyman stands behind a fake pulpit, framed by a simulated stained-glass window. For the first few seconds he stares out into the camera with a glassy-eyed look. Then he realizes that he is on camera. He launches into a meditation salvaged out of last week's sermon. He is either fighting to read while looking at the camera or rigidly reading the script above the camera. He just isn't Walter Cronkite. There is no excuse for putting him in this uncomfortable position. Stations tend to run devotions this way because it seems easier than doing something creative, and the pastors never complain. I remember calling a station to tell them that the clergyman they had been running every two weeks for the closing devotion had died two years ago.

Some creative options are being developed by restless clergymen who know that the old stand-up approach is misrepresenting the Good News to those who might be hearing the Word for the first time. In Pittsburgh there was a series of seven-minute devotions which were freshly produced by a different clergyman (Catholic, Protestant, and Jewish) each week. We would choose a person and produce the show around what he wanted to communicate. These seven, seven-minute devotions were aired at 11:30 A.M. and again after the Dick Cavett Show.

"Mirror of Faith" became an extremely rich series for the clergymen and for the audience. David Hopfer directed and produced the series. Most of the clergymen told me that this experience was among the most important of their lives. They would come with a theme or idea for their series. David would then help them explore the variety of ways by which this message could be fleshed-out in the medium of television so that the audience would be touched by it. The highly verbal tendencies of the pastors, priests, and rabbis, were softened into a visual mix. David helped the men and women think in terms of the receivers. Who are these people? How can they be touched by your message? It was amazing how many small aspects of language, voice, and gesture were really intended for the in-church community. The problem was to speak of the faith to those outside this experience. The resulting series were exciting.

For instance, Chuck Eaton utilized a number of approaches in getting at his theme: "The Answer Is Getting Clearer." The title came from a song written by some young people in the church he served. The first was entitled "Hey, Phoney." Chuck combined straight rap with a record about a Bible salesman. While the song was playing a man and woman acted out the encounter between a salesman and housewife. The host probed briefly dimensions of phoniness: selling, justice, and the church. This first show provided the setting for the following programs.

Segment two in the series was entitled: "Who Are You?" The program opened with Chuck interviewing several people with the question: "Who Are You?" Each person identified himself in a different way (name, function, skills, etc.). The pivot point of the program was an enactment of a fraternity-type exercise where people had to identify themselves as "Scum" So-and-so. Each person did this. However, the last person said: "I am Al Mossberg, for whom Jesus Christ died and was raised from the dead." This set up Chuck's rap about our identity before God.

Show three was called, "What are you worth?" The hooker here was a very clever dialogue between two people. One man asked the other what his value quotient was. He then proceeded to figure it out on a blackboard according to worldly values (income, cars, family, TV, etc.). It was done in a mock-serious manner that was both interesting and funny. He finally awarded the person being interviewed a value quotient of 2.8. Then Chuck came and stood in front of the scene and explored the question of worth.

"Give a Damn" was the title of segment four. It was built around the popular song of a few years ago. They used a slide collage to give the words visual impact. A short rap preceded and followed the music and visual experience.

Show five featured original music for the topic: "I Know the Answer Is Love." Chuck used two people from his church. They sang two songs tightly worked into his comments. The colorful set gave the show a Mike Douglas visual quality.

The sixth day's show was called "Jesus Is Just Alright." This was built upon the Byrd's popular recording from the *Easy Rider* album. Slides were again employed to give visual flesh to the message. The pictures were very sensitively selected. Chuck carefully worked to integrate the music with the message. He assumed that the audience was not familiar with the song.

Number seven concluded the series. It was called "Come on People." Music and a cast of a dozen or so people helped give body to this segment. The group slowly moved towards Chuck as he was talking. You were listening to him and at the same time felt that the community in the studio was acting out what was being said. The show concluded with the group embracing Chuck and one another while they invited the audience to come on and love their brothers.

There were aspects of the shows which could have been better. They were usually done with only one take. The station gave us three hours in the studio to do the seven shows. The crazy series of devotions received fan mail and phone calls. People were moved by the noncanned quality to the "Mirror of Faith" devotions. Each week the shows were totally different. Eventually the daily series was broadcast on several other stations in the chain owned by the television company. The series was nominated for the local media awards. The program and the station are now off the air. The results of mass-media economics.

Jerry Lackamp has been doing some interesting things with devotional programming in Cleveland. He has taken the usual sign-off and sign-on spots and developed a series of slide montages with music and/or voice over sound. These segments change according to themes. They can be paced differently with different kinds of graphic styles. Many clergymen feel more comfortable with the use of the voice than with standing before a camera.

In this section on television you may have noted that several of the program designs are no longer in existence or did not even get on the air. This is an important aspect of ministry in the electric age. In the past we have tended to relate success with longevity. Just a moment's reflection can reveal the danger in this equation. However, remember this: The message was there. The length of Jesus' ministry did not reflect its power and importance. The fact that the disciples had short ministries and sometimes shallow converts did not invalidate what they were called to do. In the realm of mass media, things come and go rapidly. Station personnel are here today and gone tomorrow. Very few national shows last more than a couple of years. If a series goes three years, it is considered a success, and those involved are fixed financially for life. In fact, a number of shows have voluntarily closed down because they were afraid of growing stale. If the church would only learn to accept the decay or fatality rate in social units, there would not be those deadly groups meeting for a hundred years. Groups should last as long as they continue to communicate what they were created to communicate. When that time has past, they should end. New forms can then grow up to provide the new wineskins for the new wine of faith.

This means that your mass media ministry may focus on a project for a few years. It can then close down and you can develop something else. This is not failure. It is just the process of maintaining a skin-close relationship between medium, the message, and the constituency. When this contact breaks down, there is no communication of the primary message left. This style of work may be likened to a tabernacling ministry. We can set up our tent where the Spirit dwells. Our faith keeps us from worshiping forms in the place of the living God. There is tension and uncertainty about what we are doing, with no neat results. We are wonderfully freed to do and be what we are called to manifest.

K. THE CHURCH AS CONVENER

The sense of totality in the midst of fragmentation is particularly needed in the electric media circus. No one is really charged with giving an overview to all the messages and programming that is being carried by the stations in your community. This means that a lot of impact slippage takes place. In one community, a local priest invited the station managers for lunch. He was simply providing them the forum for the exchange of ideas. Out of the first meeting came a community-wide media campaign against VD. Each station would approach the subject its own way. It was significant that several of the station people asked the clergyman if he could call another such meeting. As one program director explained they never got together as media people just to talk. None of them could call such a meeting. They are competing against each other, and such a move would cause suspicion.

This case suggests an important role that you and your people could play. Perhaps the ministry of reconciliation means that you bring people together in a context of warmth, in order that they may better do their job. In mass media this kind of work is vital. The church may be the only organization in the community which can do this without raising suspicion. A deep trust and respect for the convening host will result from such an activity. Your mass media committee should seriously consider this kind of approach.

L. CABLE TV

There is a new communication web spreading across the land. This new television monster is springing up in local contexts, for it is really like a giant community antenna which brings in distant stations with great clarity. These FCC-licensed cable systems are connected directly into the subscriber's home.

They also have the capacity to broadcast original community-centered programming. With the wide range of channel possibilities, special interest groups should have access to mass media in a new and exciting way.

Most of these stations have very scant equipment for these broadcasts. It is hoped that in the near future portable equipment will be available so that citizens can tape directly in the community itself. Most cable owners are very happy to have community people do programming. This helps them fulfill their public service commitment and win new subscribers. When people start talking about what happened on a locally produced show last night, those who have not signed up yet will feel that they are missing something.

There are those who believe that these new cable systems will wipe out mass network television. The network's financial interest in cable may confirm this hunch. What could happen in a community where anyone can be on television with his opinion, hobby, or concern? Wow! A revolution may be just around the corner.

The thing that stands in the way of such a revolution in human communication is creativity. Who will step forth and enable people to express themselves? Someone has to create a format in which this can take place. Someone must facilitate this process of speaking and being heard.

Eugene Leiter documents this possibility in reporting on his work as a local pastor in Janesville, Wisconsin. He established a trust relationship with Total TV, Inc. and developed a series of shows on human problems. The shows were produced in cooperation with the Ecumenical Fellowship Communications Committee. Gene and his folk really did their homework. They developed not only their programming, but they also mapped out a very complete publicity and feedback system. The shows were panel-style shows with viewers phoning in questions. The shows were well received.

The Janesville media folk then obtained the volunteer services of a college student and several high school students for a follow-up survey on the impact of the shows and of the cable TV system itself. Their sampling helped them and the station learn more about the needs of the community and also where they should go after this first probe into media ministry. The only real cost was for publicity. They purchased ads in a local paper. This case study illustrates well what we have been suggesting in terms of public media. The church can be a key factor in the process of public access to media.

There is much about cable TV which reminds one of early educational television. This was an era when insurance salesmen came off the street and ran cameras. These were the fun days of television. The production of the shows was rough and rugged. However, there was a live quality to them. Commercial television just isn't this way. Even educational television is more sophisticated now. Cable is a frontier medium waiting for folks to move in and claim it. If the church should fail to meet this challenge now, the future may be bleak. It is also possible that church should bring in the best of human resource from a large area to the local cable station. For instance, churchmen in four or five areas could work together in the production of localized programming for airing in all the stations. Local people from four different communities could talk with a Billy Graham or a William Stringfellow and have this show on the local station. This kind of intercable cooperation will have to come from someone like the churchman with these ties outside the local community.

Another hopeful thrust can be seen in the work of George Conklin and his colleagues (Conference Office, United Church of Christ, Room 671, 870 Mar Street, San Francisco, California, 94102). With about two thousand dollars worth of video-tape equipment they have been able to develop some stunning cable programming for local communities. They have been focusing on preevangelism and community building.

A good example of their work is their series on the family. Studies revealed that their local communities were quite mobile. With the swift pace of work and school, most families in these cities depended on the traditional nuclear structure as their support system. The ministry they needed was one which would give them more resources or tools to make the family relationship work. Dr. Gerald Smith developed some family relationship games which could be played by a typical unit at home. They hand-carried their camera equipment to several homes where families were playing the simulation games. The final shows featured an edited collection (assemble edit) of different families playing games of interpersonal relationships. Dr. Smith made comments about the strengths of the options chosen by the families as they played. He also reflected on the intercut segments which suggested other possibilities in dealing with the communication problems which arose in these family situations.

The twelve programs were produced for this series, and viewers were given the opportunity to play the games in their own family setting if they wished. George said that the feedback was very encouraging. Members of the families participating in the shows had a lot of people talk to them about their experience.

The cost per show, even with the use of outside enablers or producers, was quite low. The availability of the portable equipment, which the local cable station usually does not have, was very important. The shows were shot in a hand-camera style which has been most often associated with the *cinema-verite*. This "video-verite" or "truth" approach gave the shows a "people" quality which is missing from much of the slick programming one often sees on local commercial stations.

George is convinced that mass media must be demythologized if local folk are going to do electric communication. The church's fear, distrust, and awe of the electric web may undercut the possibilities that a medium like cable TV presents. George has found that the only way to get people over this gap of participation is to let them participate. These media folks like to roll up to a church with their simple equipment and have local people produce television in a couple hours. Mass media can only be related to our faith and our ministry through this skin-close experience. One doesn't learn to communicate through mass media by reading books or going to seminars. The final reality of being a Christian doing the Word via electric media is the doing. It is hard to learn the art of riding a two-wheeler without getting on the bike. There is a magical moment when you become wheel-borne. "Look at me. I'm riding." We learn to ride by riding.

George Conklin and his folk feel that there is much interest in the kind of people-media we have been championing. Business and industry know the power and possibility that reside in this release of creative local energy. It looks as if grants may be available to church folk who can get such a process together for their community. We have suggested elsewhere in this book that the co-oping existing power and resources may be the model of the future for those who want to touch human life. There are forces at work in every community which can be woven into your design without any compromise of your main objectives or theirs. Cable is an excellent occasion for probing this new style of media ministry.

The members of the California, Pennsylvania, Ministerium used their cable system to good advantage during the Lenten season. They rented a video series on biblical study for airing during the course of the five Sundays. The ministerium had to provide the technician for the show. They were able to get the aid of the person who headed the college television department. They then organized ecumenical viewing groups in the community. The shows were aired 7:30 P.M.

John Rankin quickly received an education in the technical aspects of video tape. The Bible series arrived on two-inch tape. The cable system used one-inch tape, and the first show was to be aired the next day. The pastors quickly organized a panel discussion as an introduction to the series. The personality mix was good and the show made a great impact. Meanwhile, John found that the dental school in a nearby town could make the tape dub from the two-inch to the one-inch mode. The rest of the series went off according to plan.

The community responded very positively to this use of cable TV. Norm Hunt found that eighty or more of his people had actually met in study groups around the community. A number of the ecumenical study groups decided to continue their meetings after the televised series was over.

The challenge of this freedom and opportunity will be utilization. Now that we have this new medium what are we going to do with it? Each new technology forces us to raise this question. Minority groups are now itching to express their concerns through this medium. To me, this is one of the most important aspects of people doing mass media. There is something very healing and constructive about expressing yourself in an electric format. The whole process of focusing on what you want to express, who the audience is, and how to bring message and receiver together is exciting. I have seen very angry and violent people move through a whole cycle of growth as the result of creating a powerful statement of their concerns. Cable TV offers the possibility of finding your own way of stating your case. It should not be a situation where the dissenter has to come on alien territory to express himself. Self-expression on mass media is the process of freeing yourself for more understanding and more power. This is a layer of the Good News which man needs to experience. It seems that this medium is poised to serve one of the most important aspects of Christian theology. It is just there. Who is going to see that it is used for this purpose?

VII. SUMMING UP

I think that the thrust of this book is clear: As a Christian, you are called to utilize mass media to prepare the soil in which the Good News can take root. There are several steps to this process which have emerged in the course of our discussion of radio and television.

1. *Discover your Christian identity in community.* This can best be done by gathering a cadre of folk who want to carry this understanding of evangelism to the world via mass media. Study the book of Acts. Really crawl into the Scripture (see my *Switched On Scripture* cassette series, Abingdon Audio•Graphics).

2. *Discover the nature of your mass media community.* Assign people to monitor sectors of the radio and television programming by stations. Log a typical twelve-hour period. Gather and discuss this data.

3. *Discover your local mass media people.* Divide

into teams and make contact with the station people. Get to know them and their problems. Praise them where you can honestly, by letter.

4. *Discover what is now available.* See what the national denominations can provide in terms of religious programming. Get some of the material from the Broadcast and Film Commission and practice your sensitivity by analyzing it from the perspective of what you have learned about your community.

5. *Start collecting a list of the local human resources.* This information file will be invaluable to you and the local stations.

6. *Develop support in the churches.* Prepare for an eventual publicity and feedback system in the congregation(s) to support your programming.

7. *Develop a specific programming strategy for certain stations.* These ideas should be written out and should present an outline for an actual program for that station.

8. *Get a program on the air.*

9. *Provide publicity and feedback for the program.*

10. *Work on in-church study opportunities which are related to the programming.*

11. *Work up a system of responding to those who react to the program.* If your programming brings a response from the audience, have a system ready for answering these folk. Perhaps you will want your church people to follow up what you have nurtured through mass media ministry.

12. *Convene the station managers for occasional luncheons.*

13. *Develop more programming.* Start feed-in from your file of people to the program directors on the stations.

14. *Just keep expanding on what you are doing and*

be ready to change when the Spirit and media demand.

Brothers and sisters, this is just an introduction to a realm of endless possibility. This is all much easier and, at the same time, more difficult than it seems from these comments. So has the Gospel always been. Ananias was given the truth of this when he was told that Paul would learn how much he must suffer for the sake of the Good News. It is a heavy burden I am urging you to take. However, this is the cutting edge of the faith. This is the arena in which the Word of God must be incarnate. He calls you to take this responsibility. You can do it.

VIII. CREDITS

So many folk. So many people have been shared on these pages. My two daughters, Amy and Jill, have done media with me. We have played at taping interviews. They have taken media lessons in the studio and sat on my lap while we watched their dad attempt to communicate via televised video tape. They are electric folk. Marilyn, my wife, has been the medium of love through which this media freak could become free to the new demands of the age.

So many folk. I have been taught totally by the folks with whom I have been doing media. So many mass media producers, directors, technicians, and students have led me through an education which has changed my life: Jim Sweenie, John Gibbs, David Silvian, Dick Crew, Lewis Bigler, Tom Ashwell, Mike McCormick, John Yurek, Bill Oringderff, Cliff Curley, Clayt Hartman, David Butterfield, Bob Harper, Rob McClure, Hugh Downing, Bob Mayo, Marcia Miscall, Keith Romanowski, George Erdner, Ed Willingham, Jr., Tom Bender, Charlie Brackbill, William Richards, Bob Thompson, Kenneth Haines, Lois Anderson, Bill Fore, Reuben Gums, John Bucher, Jim Quinn, Chuck Brinkman, Jay Davis, Bill Ross, and so many more.

So many folk. So many people doing creative mass media have shared their ideas and work in this book: Gene Leiter, Bud Frimoth, Frank Edmundson, Jr., Bill Huie, Sister Maureen Rodgers, Tom McLaren, Roy Humphrey, George Conklin, David Hopfer, Jack Ridl, Paul Piendl, Charles Eaton, and many members of the World Association of Christian Communicators.

So many folk. My brother David H. Barnes, has again weeded out many of the typos and other print slips in the manuscript. Mary Haynes interrupted her high school graduation celebration to get all of this typed, and Mary Jo Nickodem kindly helped in the proofreading process.

So many folk. So many members of the radio and television audience have sustained my work by tuning in and reacting. The "Rap Around" community has a special place in my heart.